More Praise for *How the Poor Can Save Capitalism*

"This book does not attempt to explain all of the economic inequality that exists in today's society but instead imagines solutions. The weakness of most theories on resolving inequality is that they do not speak to the imagination. John Bryant speaks to our imagination and delivers an inspiring message for young people that imagination and self-determination are the only tools needed to change the world. A critical reminder for Americans that there is no finality to being poor."
—**Philippe Bourguignon, Vice Chairman, Revolution Places; CEO, Exclusive Resorts; and former co-CEO, World Economic Forum**

"Economic immobility is the defining issue of America in the 21st century. John Hope Bryant makes an engaging case for why we must make our economy work for everyone. *How the Poor Can Save Capitalism* is a must-read for business leaders, policymakers, and community leaders who want to make the American Dream a reality for all our children."
—**Ben Jealous, former CEO, NAACP**

"John Hope Bryant's brilliant new book is the key to making capitalism work for everyone. Bryant writes from his heart and his personal experience as a former homeless person who has become enormously successful by investing $500 million to help the poor become financially literate *and* financially successful. Bryant's strategy and his humanity can transform society and heal the wounds that keep us apart."
—**Bill George, Professor of Management Practice, Harvard Business School, and author of *True North***

"Bryant's offering is a critically thought-out, comprehensive, and clearly articulated remedy that will advance our suffering and stymied community. And it's written beautifully and boldly from a perspective of deep understanding and compassion and a heart full of love."
—**Susan Taylor, former Editor-in-Chief, *Essence* magazine, and current CEO, National CARES Mentoring Movement**

"This book sets out a clarion call for dramatically increasing the financial capability of the undeserved and through that step encouraging their native-born instincts of entrepreneurship. Setting forth real-world examples of success from the great works of Operation HOPE, John Hope Bryant puts forth a common-sense game plan, which, if followed, will provide a better future for our nation. Let's go!"
—**Richard Ketchum, CEO, FINRA**

"John Hope Bryant is the essence of his middle name: *Hope*. A planter of the same, he invites us to cultivate by seeding hope, investing in hope, nurturing hope, and harvesting hope. He extols not a hand out, but a hand up. And what is the rope that pulls us upward? It is hope, hope such as seen in the middle class, the upward spiral that determines and differentiates between 'rich' or 'poor.' Self-determination is the new definition of freedom, and both are dependent on financial literacy. The latter provides the quartet of harmony: education, self-esteem, real choice, and real opportunity for all. This is the essence of hope. The author may be summarized in his own words: The hope factor, then, is a good job and a shot at aspirational success. Our major issue today is not so much about race, the color line, or social strife as it is about class and poverty. *Let the people say amen*."

—**Rev. Cecil L. "Chip" Murray, former Pastor, First African Methodist Episcopal Church, Los Angeles, and Tansey Chair, Center for Religion and Civic Culture, USC**

"John Hope Bryant has set out to save America by returning her to the nation's founding idea—a sustainable, growing middle class that serves as a beacon to others, a light on the hill. That's just not possible while 80 percent of the population has only 7 percent of the money. But Bryant has a plan to make free enterprise work for the poor, by providing mentors, building dignity and confidence, and enabling access to money and financial literacy. It's the right idea at the right time."

—**Sean Cleary, Member of the Board, The Abraaj Group, and Vice Chair, FutureWorld Foundation**

"John Hope Bryant's third book is finely focused on the causes of the dearth of financial literacy and the needed tactics to improve it through education and inspiration of both adults and children in the United States and other countries. A financially educated and inspired public will make better decisions in both their personal and working lives, which will yield a stronger economy and more broad-based opportunities for everyone. While I certainly don't agree with the positions of some of the people noted in the book, the achievement of John Hope Bryant's recommendations will likely require the broadest possible participation and support. This book proposes solutions, goals, and opportunities for us all to be part of the needed work."

—**Jim Wells, former CEO, SunTrust Banks**

"The greatest leaders of America have been about dignity. Abraham Lincoln ended slavery, but less known is that just before his death he founded the Freedman's Savings Bank to empower former slaves economically. Martin Luther King, Jr., was not only about civil rights—he was assassinated when he started his Poor People's Campaign for all races. In this book, John Hope Bryant lays out an inspiring and concrete plan on how to realize the unfinished vision of Lincoln and King. This book is not only to be read but to be implemented. This book operationalizes dignity in the economic field."

—**Professor Pekka Himanen, cofounder, Global Dignity**

"John Hope Bryant's work on the flaws of capitalism and what can be done about them not only is very timely but also responds to a growing global hunger for a more responsible and equitable model. His accessible style, personal reflection, and heartfelt commitment to driving change make this a must-read for all those who care about the future and a practical guide for policymakers and leaders. For too long we have overlooked our interdependency and the true value of human capital—Bryant makes an eloquent and rational call for us to put poverty and inequality right back at the top of the agenda."

—**Clare Woodcraft, CEO, Emirates Foundation**

HOW THE POOR
CAN SAVE CAPITALISM

HOW THE POOR CAN SAVE CAPITALISM

REBUILDING THE PATH
—— to the ——
MIDDLE CLASS

John Hope Bryant

BK

Berrett–Koehler Publishers, Inc.
San Francisco
a BK Currents book

Berrett-Koehler Publishers, Inc.
235 Montgomery Street, Suite 650
San Francisco, CA 94104-2916
Tel: (415) 288-0260   Fax: (415) 362-2512   www.bkconnection.com

Ordering Information

Quantity sales. Special discounts are available on quantity purchases by corporations, associations, and others. For details, contact the "Special Sales Department" at the Berrett-Koehler address above.

Individual sales. Berrett-Koehler publications are available through most bookstores. They can also be ordered directly from Berrett-Koehler: Tel: (800) 929-2929; Fax: (802) 864-7626; www.bkconnection.com.

Orders for college textbook/course adoption use. Please contact Berrett-Koehler: Tel: (800) 929-2929; Fax: (802) 864-7626.

Orders by U.S. trade bookstores and wholesalers. Please contact Ingram Publisher Services, Tel: (800) 509-4887; Fax: (800) 838-1149; E-mail: customer.service@ ingrampublisherservices.com; or visit www.ingrampublisherservices.com/Ordering for details about electronic ordering.

Berrett-Koehler and the BK logo are registered trademarks of Berrett-Koehler Publishers, Inc.

Printed in the United States of America

Berrett-Koehler books are printed on long-lasting acid-free paper. When it is available, we choose paper that has been manufactured by environmentally responsible processes. These may include using trees grown in sustainable forests, incorporating recycled paper, minimizing chlorine in bleaching, or recycling the energy produced at the paper mill.

Library of Congress Cataloging-in-Publication Data
Bryant, John Hope.
    How the poor can save capitalism : rebuilding the path to the middle
class / John Hope Bryant. -- First Edition.
       pages cm
    ISBN 978-1-62656-032-1 (hardback)
    1. Middle class--United States--Social conditions. 2. Poor--Employment--United States.
3. Economic development--United States. I. Title.
HT690.U6B793   2014
305.5'50973—dc23   2014003014

First Edition
18   17   16   15   14   LSI   10   9   8   7   6   5   4   3   2   1

Book producer and text designer: BookMatters, Berkeley, CA
Copyeditor: Todd Manza
Proofreader: Nancy Evans
Indexer: Leonard Rosenbaum
Cover designer: Kirk DouPonce, DogEared Design

This book is dedicated to the unfinished agenda of Dr. Martin Luther King Jr. and his strategist in the movement for human dignity and empowerment, my personal hero Ambassador Andrew Young. Dr. King's efforts for the Poor People's Campaign was cut short by an assassination, before it ever had a chance to rise up and engage a nation's better angels.

CONTENTS

FOREWORD

John Hope Bryant has made a wonderful, original, and visionary contribution for all of those who want to see economic inequality shrink in their lifetime. Business executives take note and follow the steps in this book! Every high school senior or college freshman should read this book. And every teacher who's teaching economics or religion also must read this book. John Bryant has condensed more information and experience in a couple of hundred pages than most any other book I've recently read.

What he says is not new, but it's presented in a fashion that is not primarily academic or intellectual. Nor is it simply a collection of business models and statistics. It really is quite prophetic.

This book is in the tradition of John Maynard Keynes's *The Economic Consequences of the Peace*, written in 1919 and ignored until the Marshall Plan was proposed in 1947. It is in the tradition of University of Michigan professor C. K. Prahalad, who wrote about *The Fortune at the Bottom of the Pyramid*. It is in the tradition of Muhammad Yunus, the "poor people's banker," and the Grameen Bank experience in Bangladesh. And John reminds us most of all that America is a summary of all of these economic thinkers as well as the vision of Isaiah springing with hope eternal from the ashes of a destroyed Jerusalem.

John Bryant used to worry me to death. And then suddenly I realized it was not worry; it was a warning. He was calling me to life. And he was calling me to realize that one cannot afford to slow down or be tired, even after eighty years of struggle. I realized that there is too much to do, that there is an urgency in today's economy and on today's planet that can only be answered with the energy and vitality inherent in youth and the experience and wisdom inherent in old age, combining to create a courageous new world order.

As mayor of Atlanta I learned that, as far as cities are concerned, national economies are mostly irrelevant. To survive, cities must join together in a global economy. And technology, which transcends borders, is far more powerful than any laws created by councils, legislators, or Congress.

John Bryant is a man born into the world of the local streets and alleys of Watts and Atlanta who now walks into parlors with presidents and princes and probably talks to a greater variety of important people in a week than most CEOs do in a year. That's because he talks to important people not only in the suites but also in the streets. And his ideas have come not through our universities or the inherited ideas of the European free market but from the strivings and struggles of small business and church neighborhoods like the one he grew up in.

I'm fascinated by the impact that John's experience as a *Soul Train* teenage dancer had on his life. If there's one thing that inspires self-esteem, confidence, and rhythm, it's dancing. It's not only John's dancing on *Soul Train* but also a young

David dancing around the Ark of the Covenant and Nelson Mandela toyi-toying his way to freedom in South Africa. Life is a dance. And when we are filled with rhythm and vitality we constantly exude hope and optimism, making all things possible. There is no such thing as failure. One must follow Frank Sinatra's example and pick ourselves up and get back in the race, because that's life.

That makes John an artist as well as a businessman. But he is a businessman who is not interested in generating personal wealth but in helping to awaken the vitality and the idealism of the world's poor, to integrate them and their entrepreneurial energy, along with their consumer power. John's hope is to revitalize the global economy of the twenty-first century.

There is more wealth in today's world than has ever existed in history. There is a greater capacity for, creation of, and access to technology than ever before—technology ranging from satellites orbiting the earth to geologic soundings in the depths of the sea, technology that proves that almost everything and anything is possible. At the same time, there is also a greater understanding of the world's needs than ever before. We can predict droughts and we can analyze the failure of the earth's surface to regenerate its topsoil, as Howard Buffett reminds us in his book *Forty Chances*.

The energy and vitality that John Bryant brings to life, the whirling dervish of energy and aggressiveness, is not that of a folk seeker but of a watchman who sees the distant dangers of chaos resulting from massive numbers of unemployed youth in our central cities and in the alleys of Delhi, and in the rural storms emerging among China's poor. He is a watchman who sees the terrorism that plagues the Middle East and the restlessness among the masses in Brazil, South Africa, Nigeria, and Russia.

He has experienced firsthand the statistics that Jim Clifton records in his prophetic book *The Coming Jobs War*, which says that a planet of seven billion people cannot be sustained with only 1.2 billion jobs, that the very survival of humanity, rich and poor alike, depends on finding ways to mobilize, innovate, generate another one billion or two billion jobs. Jobs cannot be created by wars or by governments. Jobs must somehow evolve through the interaction of vision, need, energy, and even a little greed. But greed alone only produces the wealth of the rich young ruler who, after gathering his riches into barns, was confronted by the reality that "this night thy soul is required of thee."

John Bryant is pointing to a choice between judgment and jubilee. And I think Dr. King would be proud of his efforts to inspire us to feed the hungry, clothe the naked, heal the sick, set at liberty those who are oppressed, and, in the process, create and enjoy the abundant life that the Bible promises for all of God's children.

Andrew Young
former UN ambassador,
civil rights organizer,
and mayor of Atlanta

This book is about saving America. All of America. Not black folks or Asian, Latino, or Native American folks. It's not about white folks. It's about all of us. As I make the case here, whether you are black, white, red, brown, or yellow, increasingly everyone just wants to see some more green—U.S. currency, that is.

Dr. Martin Luther King Jr. said that the movement of his day and age was intended to "redeem the soul of America from the triple evils of racism, war, and poverty." Interestingly enough, Dr. King's work also was not about black people per se. African-Americans just happened to be at the tip of the spear in the era that began in 1958. Dr. King and my mentor, former UN Ambassador Andrew Young, genuinely thought that we make America better, stronger, more resilient, more valuable, and more valued when the nation has the benefit of everyone rowing in the waters of prosperity, dignity, and human aspiration. By 1968 Dr. King had turned his attention to a Poor People's Campaign that involved and sought to engage the whole of America, every race. The reality is that there are more poor white people in America than poor anyone else.

This book focuses on the challenges and, more important,

the economic opportunity for America. Not opportunity for the 99 percent or the 1 percent but opportunity for the 100 percent that makes up our collective whole and our strength as a nation. By extension, I hope to inspire a generation of leaders, here and around the world, to act on things they might have previously thought unsolvable.

We step into a minefield of perspective and controversy when we say we set out to radically reimagine the solution to poverty. And we go even further when we seek to redefine our collective understanding of poverty itself. This book is meant to be bold, to turn so-called social and societal norms on their heads.

My radical reimagining of the definition of poverty is what I call the HOPE Doctrine on Poverty. This approach to defining poverty is a departure from the status quo, because the current definition, respectfully, misses the point completely. It is limited by its sole commitment to numbers. But if we restrict the notion of poverty to a purely statistical interpretation, as our government is understandably required to do, we miss the human element.

As I speak about poverty, I am an outlier. In so doing, there are some things I am *not* going to do:

- I don't intend to argue about absolutes.

- I am not an economist. I do not hold a degree in economics. So I don't intend to opine on academic theory. We have enough credible theory already in circulation, and this is not an economics textbook or an academic treatise.

- This is not polemic intended to stake a claim to philosophical territory. I do not hold a degree in philosophy, either.

And let me make this clear: this book is not about social-ism, and it is definitely not about communism. Communism has failed completely, and socialism simply cannot work in the United States. Government has its place in our society, but we must all remember that 92 percent of all jobs in the United States come from the private sector. Even China, a communist country, has chosen capitalism. I have come to believe that capitalism is a horrible system—except for every other system. And no one has ever tried to make free enterprise and capital-ism work for the poor and others left out and left behind in America, at scale.

This book is nothing if not practical. And so is my defini-tion of poverty. After growing up as part of the teetering class in South Central Los Angeles and Compton, California; after being homeless at the age of eighteen; and after working over the past twenty-two years with everyone from the working poor to the working class to the struggling middle class, in the offices of Operation HOPE, I feel as though I understand modern poverty.

The HOPE Doctrine on Poverty says that there are three things that define poverty and struggle more than any set of financial numbers ever could: self-confidence, self-esteem, and belief in oneself; role models and environment; aspiration and opportunity. Or the lack of these things.

Self-confidence, self-esteem, and belief in oneself. In this country, if you wake up in the morning and you don't know who you are, by dinnertime someone will tell you who you are. If you don't have self-confidence, you are in serious trouble in America—and maybe anywhere.

Role models and environment. Think about your family and your immediate community. If your role models are negative, the only aspiration you see around you is illegal, and if your immediate environment stinks, then your well-being is going to take a real hit.

When we think about this, why is anyone surprised if inner-city youth grow up wanting to be rap stars or athletes—with no disrespect intended to either of these professions—or, unfortunately, drug dealers? Life is very simple: you model what you see. These kids are not dumb; they are brilliant. They are modeling what they see.

Finally, life is about aspiration and opportunity. If you don't have the opportunity, the chance, the shot at operationalizing your smarts, your talents, or your education, then life has a concrete ceiling rather than a glass one. You feel that all is for naught, so why try in the first place? You lose hope, and the most dangerous person in the world is a person without hope.

Harvesting in the Plot of the Poor

As I look for real, sustainable solutions to the poverty and lack of opportunity I see every day during my work at Operation HOPE, I have come to a strange conclusion: We have most likely locked up and thrown away the key to some of the very character traits that are required to stand up a community, create an emerging market and jobs, and grow local economies. We have actually tossed away the portion of society that we need to save it, leaving the elderly, the infirm, the young, broken families, or the traditional job striver to save a faltering community.

What would happen if all of these otherwise brilliant young people, whose main role models for "success" in their communities are drug dealers, rap stars, or athletes, instead were given a proper business role model or a business internship? Maybe it would change everything.

It did for me.

There is a complete disconnect of the capitalist system from "the least of these," and this disconnect weakens the system for the very people who think the poor aren't their problem. Locking people out—denying them access to information, finance, and opportunity—is what happens when capitalism is lazy. Retreating behind our gates is what happens when capitalism is scared. On the other hand, a harvest in the plot of the poor is what can happen if we are all willing to do the real, sustainable, transformational work that builds a nation.

Harvesting in the plot of the poor has two sides. We invest our time and our finance, yes, and our investment may be based on our beliefs and desires, but we must also respect that the plot itself belongs to the poor, the underserved, the struggling classes. That plot may contain only their ideas or their sweat equity in the form of time, energy, and commitment to advancement, but whatever it is, it must be respected as theirs. It must be valued, and it is valuable.

What I am talking about is creating an amazing bumper crop that sends gross domestic product and the stock exchange through the roof, and that is as American as apple pie. In fact, *it's a pie that creates more pie.* But to get that pie, we must first plant, water, nurture, and harvest the apples.

The fact is, we have done this before. This humble cultivation of and commitment to finding everyone's talent is where

America began. We have not always been well-to-do or able to walk away from ourselves and each other. We once needed each other. Desperately so. America the beautiful as we now know it was once made up of the broke and the under-resourced, a mostly immigrant population that came here to escape oppression and a limited life somewhere else. This is something to remember, by the way, when someone is talking about those "illegals." America is a grab bag of immigrant vagabonds from the world over, and a majority of her most amazing entrepreneurship success stories are also stories of struggling immigrants. These are the people who produced a country that is now the envy of people all over the world who *still* want to come here.

But we have been comfortably riding this wave for far too long, and now it is time to produce a new harvest.

Andrew Young often says to me, "Men fail for three reasons: arrogance, pride, and greed." All three of these things are rooted in insecurity and fear, and doing the wrong or utterly selfish thing most often happens when fear and insecurity overtake our being, our inner reason. The key to winning is to get over these insecurities and fears, to first conquer ourselves and to learn to become reasonably comfortable in our own skins. I cannot like you, love you, or respect you unless I like, love, and respect myself first. But the dangerous other side of this is also true: if I don't have a purpose in my life, I am going to make your life a living hell. The poor and the underserved must be given a stake in this thing we call America or I promise you they will tear it up—right before they tear it down. This is not an alarmist statement. The most dangerous person in the world is a person with no hope.

So I am not suggesting that we cultivate the plot of the poor because it is morally right, even though it is, but because it just makes good, sustainable sense. We must do it because it is the only thing left to do that has half a chance of working and of benefiting both the powerful and the dispossessed alike. Far from being a dilemma, then, the decision to include the poor is both obvious and necessary. Unless we want to hand over to our children a world that has simply come off the rails of sanity, it is in the enlightened self-interest of us all to make the right decisions now.

This book is about saving America and returning her to her original promise, her original founding ideas and ideals. It is about planting, nurturing, and growing a sustainable middle class, creating once again what my friend Steve Bartlett, former president and CEO of the Financial Services Roundtable, calls a "light on the hill." This is a place where the new, twenty-first-century definition of freedom is expressed as self-determination—the opportunity that comes from one's own hands and one's own bold ideas connected to action, personal risk, personal investment, and hard work. This book is about creating a new, sustainable business plan that returns this country to its original big, bold, audacious dream. This idea is both utterly liberal and the very definition of conservative at the same time.

If I give a homeless man a million dollars, there's a pretty good chance he will be broke and homeless once again in, say, six months, because he has not been given the additional nurturing or resources that would enable him to create a different path for himself. Sympathy has its place, and pure charity is absolutely necessary and essential, maybe more so today than at any time in recent history. But only an intelligently applied approach of empathy, rather than a liberally spread dose of sympathy, is sustainable with respect to national policy and a competitive market economy.

America is not a country; it is an idea. And we can reimagine it to be anything we like.

PART I

SEEDING HOPE

CHAPTER ONE

Separate, Unequal America

I am aiming to turn upside down some "truths" about the economy, jobs, where wealth comes from, and who stands to gain the most if we tap the armies of ignored and "inconvenient" poor and working poor who are presently left on the sidelines. We have some big problems and challenges to address, but despite what we might hear on the evening news, the United States remains the largest economy in the world, at approximately $16 trillion in annual gross domestic product.[1] Our best years are not behind us. We have enormous human resources of wealth creation and opportunity just waiting to be unleashed.

The future of our economic story fully depends on overturning these powerful myths about how the economy works for the rich, the poor, the middle class, and everyone in between. We are all called to leave our comfortable assumptions and to arrest the crumbling of the American dream that built this country in the first place.

For instance, consumers—not businesses or governments—power the bulk of our massive economy, with fully 70 percent of the economy dependent on consumer spending.[2] This means that you and I are driving the largest economy in the world, by purchasing everything from iced cappuccinos to ice shovels, from gas to put in our cars to the cars themselves. Sustained economic growth and the fortunes of the other 30 percent of the economy represented by businesses and governments, therefore, depends on the economic vibrancy of ordinary consumers, most of whom are not wealthy.

Even so, these ordinary Americans are much more reliable spenders than the wealthy; the bottom 80 percent of the American workforce spends 90 percent of its income, whereas the wealthiest 1 percent spends only 49 percent.[3] The average American cannot afford *not* to spend the bulk of his or her paycheck on the basic necessities of living, but the rich simply make too much to spend it all. Ordinary Americans are the coal that feeds our economic locomotive, and if Wall Street, banks, and large corporations are going to make their numbers and increase their wealth, they need this segment of the economy to become more economically strong and stable. This invariably means expanding opportunity through well-paying jobs and small businesses, along with financial inclusion and know-how.

But the "bottom" 80 percent of consumers, the backbone of the economy, owns only 11 percent of the nation's money.[4] We're now building the consumer-driven 70 percent of our economic growth on the backs of those who have only a 7 percent stake in the system, and as many as ten million of these consumer households don't even have a bank account.[5] When the poor, the underserved, and the struggling middle class start feeling uneasy about the future, or when they are out of work or out of money, they stop spending on consumer products. And when they stop doing this, everything else stops as well.

The people driving our economy get little regard, less respect, and almost no consideration for doing so. Although the system works well for some, it is leaving many behind, and as a result it is understandably coming to an end.

What might happen if we instead place faith and confidence in and support those who can actually lift our economy—who already do, through their consumer spending alone? Just imagine if we viewed the poor as something other than a tool to be used, taken advantage of, and taken for granted. What if we actually valued the poor? After all, the rich need the poor, if for no other reason than to remain rich themselves.

Helping the Poor to Transform America

We must value the poor and, through them, transform America. As Dr. King said in his 1964 Nobel lecture, "No individual or nation can be great if it does not have a concern for 'the least of these.'" Dr. King was referring to Matthew 25:40, where Jesus said, "Inasmuch as ye have done it unto one of the least of these my brethren, ye have done it unto me." I believe Dr. King was both morally correct and economically profound.

We don't have to settle for capitalism the way we have it, or the way it's been. We can refashion and reimagine capitalism as we would have it, and then do something other than complain about it. We can finally make free enterprise and capitalism actually work for the poor, the struggling classes, and the least of God's children. The world has never tried it at scale, but this is precisely my plan. In this plan, everyone gets a role to play, not just the president and other elected officials, big business, or big banks. This is our country, our world, and our communities, and if change is to come, we must drive that change.

Reimagining the Poor

So the first myth that we need to overturn is the idea that poor people are somehow not relevant to our economic growth. The second myth is that the poor somehow did this to themselves—that they are all bums and deserve to be poor because they're lazy, have bad habits, or possess a horrible work ethic. Our logic then follows: "Why should I help someone who deserves what they got?" That would make perfect sense, if it were true.

Even I used to think this way. Growing up black in the inner city, in a diverse neighborhood of striving and struggling families, attending public school, I had to find a way to deal with all the dynamics that came my way on a daily basis, to deal with difficult people, and to negotiate myself out of almost any tough situation. I was never the biggest kid, or the toughest, and, unlike the rich of this nation, I could not build the equivalent of a gate around my existence, so I had to try to be the smartest kid. One of the ways I dealt with what I saw, then, was through rationalization. I thought I understood poverty. I convinced myself that the poor people I saw were all bums and I had a dozen reasons to be against them. I now know I was wrong, and I also know that to rationalize is to tell rational lies. I was only fooling myself. And this is the worst deceit.

What I didn't understand was all the external factors that helped me to avoid becoming one of "them." I had a mother who told me she loved me and a father who was the role model I needed to see in business. I had a banker come into my classroom when I was nine years old and unpack the mysterious world of free enterprise and capitalism, explaining to me the "language of money," financial literacy. I was so totally focused on dreams and was so hopeful about my future that I seldom noticed the actual causes of all the drama and mayhem that surrounded me on a daily basis—lack of financial literacy, lack of access to banking and credit, lack of real estate ownership, lack of role models and opportunity. Lack of self-esteem.

I didn't get out because I was the brightest or most talented kid on my block. I knew plenty of brighter, more talented kids who ended up on an economic dead end or even just plain dead. I got out and did well because of the hope factor that surrounded and encompassed my life. But when this magic doesn't happen in a kid's life, and when the factors that actually drain opportunity happen often enough, then kids begin to lose hope. And the most dangerous person in the world is a person with no hope.

When enough people are deprived of hope often enough and for long enough periods of time, then a community's culture itself gets hijacked. Hijacked by thugs and thug culture. Hijacked by all the elements and the operators who seize on and even live on that loss of hope. Over time, people, cultures, and communities respond internally to how they are treated externally. Tell someone they aren't valuable or important and, in time, far too many of them begin to believe it.

Recreating a Pathway to the Middle Class

A poverty of hope cannot be solved with a nice apartment, a new car, or even a new school building in a neighborhood. This problem has to be attacked from all sides to prevent a self-perpetuating cycle in which the very poverty of the poor seems to justify the poverty itself, in which we come to think of the poor as noncontributing members of society who somehow did it to themselves.

In order to do this, we need to recapture that old hope that if you work hard, keep your nose clean, go to school and get good grades, pay your taxes and your emotional dues, it will pay off in a fair shot at the American dream and your children will have a legitimate shot at living an even better life than you. Today, both of these dreams seem to be shattered, not for just the poor and the underserved but also for the struggling middle class. Today, the bet seems to be off, or even lost, and the crisis that is spreading now is really more of a loss of confidence than a loss of net worth or home equity.

People don't mind taking risks and losing a little, maybe even a lot, as long as they believe there is still a legitimate shot at the dream. People don't mind that the lucky, fortunate, and hard-working get rich, because to be blunt and honest, they all want to be rich too. The problem arises when people begin to believe that the game is rigged, that no matter what they do they simply cannot get ahead. That is when a healthy skepticism turns into a destructive cynicism.

There are increasingly few or no clear pathways to the middle class, but unfortunately, most unaffected people do not care. Poverty was not debated or even substantially spoken about in the most recent presidential election. It is out of vogue to discuss the poor, much less to be poor. And even among those who want to help, the answer is all too often, "I would love to help, as long as the solution doesn't increase my taxes, cause me inconvenience, or happen in my backyard."

But we should all care, because the fate of the poor is the fate of us all.

Consider Detroit, Michigan, which recently filed for bankruptcy. Fifty years ago Detroit was an economic hub, a center of culture and manufacturing jobs, home of some of the largest industries, companies, and employers in the world, supplying American-made automobiles to a burgeoning American middle class. Stable jobs, good wages, and benefits fueled a thriving middle class, and families and neighborhoods flourished. Back then, Detroit was the fourth-largest city in the nation, with more than two million residents, and boasted the largest per capita income in America.

Today, the entire automobile industry is a shell of its former self, and after decades of decay and retreat, the population of Detroit has declined to about seven hundred thousand and the unemployment rate stands at more than 18 percent. Those stable, high-paying jobs have been replaced by technology and global competition, resulting in a complete collapse of the economy.

This wasn't the fault of the workers. Instead, Detroit's leaders lost sight of that story line, and a city about the many, which found a magical way to ride a wave up, increasingly became a city about the few, where everyone concerned rode the original dream into a deep fiscal ditch. The leaders forgot about the struggling class that made the city in the first place. Detroit made things and Detroit remade things but Detroit didn't reimagine things as they could be, rather than just the way things happen to be today.

For instance, the original mission, vision, and purpose of the trade unions in Detroit was workers standing together to protect themselves and ensure a decent standard of living. But today most people in Detroit could not actually tell you what that original mission was. Instead, the unions began to see their role as simply guaranteeing jobs, raises, and benefits, to the point that worker health insurance is today one of the largest expenses for a Detroit car manufacturer. General Motors planned to spend more than $60 billion on employee health insurance, an average of $1,400 per automobile coming off the line.[6] Its biggest expenditure would thus be employee benefits, not a new-technology engine that runs on alternative fuel or a newly designed emissions system to reduce carbon dioxide levels.

Detroit went broke long before it went bust; it ran out of ideas. This isn't the fault of the poor, but this is one of the reasons the poor stay poor, and it is one of the reasons that Detroit became the largest municipal bankruptcy case in American history.

Or consider Chicago, a city on the bubble and simultaneously at a radical hundred-year tipping point. It could go either way—it could become a model for breakthrough transformation of cities or it could crater. Chicago is an economic engine of the Midwest, home to countless Fortune 1,000 companies, yet Chicago is today a tale of two cities. There is the posh Chicago, which is a national tourist mecca, and the other Chicago, which locals call "Chi-raq"—a locked-down, suffocating war zone where forty-five young people from urban, low-wealth communities were shot or stabbed in one weekend.[7]

Chicago's leadership is understandably throwing everything it can at the problem, from increased law enforcement to stronger sentencing to traditional summer youth employment options. In other words, their solutions are both reactionary and visionary, both fear-based and aspiration-based. But the current crop of aspirational incentives is not very aspirational. Instead, they are merely functional. And that's a problem.

No powerful trade union or law enforcement agency can keep a city's economy alive by itself. Likewise, cities don't thrive because of law enforcement, although civilized society requires both. Cities thrive when there is a high level of individual economic energy and at least the perception of enough opportunity to go around. And all of this is about one thing: hope made real through a pathway to the middle class. This requires an allowance and an opportunity for everyone to become a stakeholder in that city's dream. Not a creditor to the dream, not a supplicant, usurper, or bottom fisher to the dream, but a stakeholder, a participant, a partner in that dream. It's not what we get but what we have to give that matters most.

If we want to save America, we must save its cities, and the only way to save America's cities is with a vibrant and believable pathway to the middle-class American dream. Middle-class people and families don't want war or strife, they want to go shopping! Actually, they just want economic opportunity. The best stabilizer of societies, here and around the world, is not twenty-year-olds armed with AK-47 assault rifles but ten- and fifteen-year-olds armed with hope, economic energy, opportunity, and a dream of a life better than their parents. Currently, the economic energies of the poor are neglected or wasted. They're outside the system.

Teaching the Language of Money

It's time for a rebirth of America, in America, by America. It's time for us to reimagine everything. Currently, we are comfortable helping the poor with philanthropy, government assistance, or microfinance, but these solutions are all inadequate. The poor don't just need "help"; they need investment. They need to be treated as customers and job creators. The main driver of freedom in the world today is not the vote but access to capital and knowledge about how to use it (self-determination). That means financial literacy education, financial capability, and financial and economic empowerment. If people don't understand the global language of money, and if they don't have a bank or credit union account, they are simply an economic slave. Thus, access to finance and financial literacy is a new civil rights issue.

I have gotten to this point of my life precisely because of the rights restored to me from and through the original civil rights movement here in America. I was able to dream big dreams as a child because of the struggle, sacrifices, and investment made by my mother, my father, my uncles and aunts, my grandparents and great-grandparents, and others. I had great role models. But this history and these people could not completely help me to get to the place I wanted to go next, the place where the poor, the underserved, and the struggling classes need to go next.

The poor and the underserved have never gotten a memo, a manual, or any education in free enterprise and responsible capitalism. Poor neighborhoods and communities simply make the rules up as they go. It's not surprising that these communities have fallen behind; the amazing part is that they have done a pretty impressive job of this thing with no help, almost no guidance, and zero role modeling of real wealth creation. Unfortunately, the vast majority of these economic shortcuts implode in time.

My father, the businessman that I modeled most growing up, got up early every day, worked all day, often six days a week, got home late. He also employed other people and was the very definition of "hard work." At one point he owned a small business, a gas station, an eight-unit apartment building, even our home.

He also ran a concrete contracting company, laying driveways and building the most beautiful brick walls. But he had a unique way of bidding jobs. He just underbid whoever was there right before him, which meant that while my father got the most jobs, he also lost the most money. For every dollar he made he spent roughly $1.50, which meant that the more money he made the more broke our family became.

After fifty-five years of running a business this way, my dad ended his amazing career dead broke. After a career of hard work, saving, and sacrifice, he lost everything. He knew all about hard work but he had learned almost nothing about the language of money, financial literacy. And not only did we lose everything but also our family fell apart. My mom and dad divorced; my brother never got to go to college. My dad made a series of bad financial moves, which in time and like dominoes ultimately derailed all of our life aspirations. But this wasn't entirely his fault.

This is only one, personal example. There are countless stories of the once poor and now famous rap star or the professional athlete with a multimillion-dollar contract. These superstars earn the money, but when it comes to figuring out what to do with it, they are winging it. And winging it, with a one-shot opportunity at that kind of money, generally works out very badly. Sixty percent of NBA players and an alarming 78 percent of NFL players will file for bankruptcy within five years of retirement.[8]

Or look at the guys who sell drugs and eventually find that their only real assets include a cool wardrobe, a hot car (with horrible financing attached), and a roll of dollar bills burning a hole in their pockets. They don't own real estate, they have no savings, and in most cases, they don't even have a bank account. They're essentially living an expensive, high-gloss version of hand to mouth.

When young people are not given financial education, and when schools don't seem to connect the power of education with the power of aspiration, those young people understandably start looking for shortcuts to financial success. And when such shortcuts are modeled on the high-profile shortcuts people see on TV or the things they see in their communities, they are likely to be headed for the strongest and most painful failure. None of this stuff works in the long term. It just feels good in the moment. It is the very definition of winning battles and losing wars.

This ripples outward in a self-perpetuating cycle. Many American communities exhibit this short-term, get-it-now, looks-like-success-so-it-must-be-so version of winging it, at scale. Add a thugged-out culture that is increasingly dropping out of school and simultaneously losing hope and you have a prescription for an American societal crisis within twenty years.

It is simply not sustainable, and all of it feeds and feeds on hopelessness. What we need now is a reset, and a new business plan based on real financial literacy.

The Freedom of Self-Determination

But financial literacy, access to credit and banking, is not enough without opportunity. In the twentieth century, the definition of freedom was tied to what was going on in the wider world—a handful of defining movements toward emerging democracies, led by leaders such as Michael Collins in Ireland, Mahatma Gandhi in India, and the late Nelson Mandela in South Africa. The United States, of course, has been blessed with leaders such as Julian Bond, Amelia Boynton, Medgar Evers, Marian Wright Edelman, Dr. Dorothy I. Height, the Reverend Leon H. Sullivan, Dr. King, Congressman John Lewis, A. Philip Randolph, the Reverend C. T. Vivian, Andrew Young, and Whitney Young, leading a homegrown civil rights movement.

In each of these places, the primary issue was race, the color line, and social strife, and the cure was almost always democracy and the right to vote, which in turn ultimately triggered real changes in public leadership, important laws, and the public policy governing fundamental issues of fairness and fair play. Looking back on the twentieth century, I think it is fair to say that democracy indeed won this fight.

Democracy continues to fight the good fight in parts of the world that are not yet free to vote, dream, or create on their own. But the issues faced today in much of the world are different. Today, the new definition of freedom is self-determination.

I was recently a passenger in a Washington, DC, car service owned and operated by a Pakistani-born man who had immigrated to the United States, quickly building a family and an entirely new life. When I asked him why he had come to the United States, risking so much to get here, leaving behind his life and family back at home, his answer was one word: *freedom*. Then I asked why he had picked this particular business, which was probably not going to make him rich and in which, like my father, he worked long hours, sometimes weekends, often holidays. Again, the answer was simple, instantaneous, and one word: *freedom*.

This man did not come to America to get rich; he came here for a feeling. He was running his own small business—the heart of the American dream—to make a living, yes, but more importantly, so that he could do as he liked, when he liked, however he liked. He could choose who entered his car as a client, who stayed, and even who came back. He had an option to take one vacation with his family in a year or to work a few more days in a month and take two vacations in that same year.

He enjoyed a number of other benefits, too. He could send his child to public school in a free nation or he could work a little harder and send that same child to private school. Later he might choose to send them to a college or university. He was not focused on growing his business a given percent per annum, accumulating a certain amount of wealth in his bank account, or attaining a particular quantifiable return on equity. Instead, he was focused on living his version of the American dream—a life that is self-determined.

This sense of self-determination begins with financial dignity. We must move from a legacy of civil rights justice for a few to what I call "silver rights" empowerment for all. Ensuring financial literacy and economic opportunity is the new civil rights issue for this generation, and the real underlying solution, in troubled places both here and around the world, is to create job opportunities—and not just government-sponsored jobs. Some of these jobs will be broadly based, from private sector jobs to newly minted corporate jobs for the college trained. But even more important are the small business jobs and the magical power of entrepreneurship that creates jobs.

We must move one hundred million or more Americans (approximately one-third of the U.S. population) up and into true participation in the free enterprise system, anchored with education, self-esteem, real choice, and real opportunity for all. I not only want rich and poor people alike to think for themselves, I also want them to think differently. I want them to reimagine everything and then to go and do something about it in their lives. This is what I mean when I talk about wealth. This is about delivering the memo to families who never got one.

Restoring Hope

Giving people financial literacy and an opportunity for self-determination means giving them hope. But the reverse is also true: making this country work for the masses of struggling

Americans, the middle class, and those who want to one day join them depends on the power of hope itself. Hope is so powerful that you only need a super minority of it to change the world. Indeed, Shane Lopez, a leading social scientist measuring the impact and power of hope, found that hope is a greater indicator of academic success and graduation rates than ACT and GPA scores combined.[9]

The hope factor, as I describe it, is the general feeling that if you follow the rules it will pay off with an opportunity for success or failure on your own merit. When the average person no longer believes this is the case, then all bets are off and all of society is screwed. At the end of the day, this is not an economic crisis in America; it is a crisis of virtues and values. It's not what we are doing but what we are about.

No one succeeds in the long term and no society can achieve long-term sustainable success by remaining focused on what it is against. The soaring rhetoric of our Constitution, our Bill of Rights, and even our best business plans are all "what I am for" sort of stuff. It's all built on hope and the intangibles of belief.

What poor folks need now is action and a plan based on what America is for in a world expert at figuring out what it is against. We must be for and work toward financial literacy and access for all. We must be in favor of providing people with the education and opportunity to discover and follow their own paths to self-determination.

Just think of the magic that the Occupy Wall Street movement could have worked if it had done more than simply channel a generational frustration with capitalism. Think about the power of developing an alternative economic system and then placing that bold, practical, and compelling vision before America. There was a moment when they would have had nothing but buyers for that dream. Even the media was looking for something it could print about an agenda that a generation could be for and then an action plan to do something to accomplish it.

It may have been a missed opportunity, but that opportunity still exists. We must harness hope by shifting from stating what we are against to working toward what we are for, and that alone will create positive economic energy. That alone changes the tone and culture of the environment in which we live and lifts us all up. Black poverty, white poverty, it's all poverty.

CHAPTER TWO

A New Look at Income Disparity

The poor are not who we might think they are. The traditional government method of gauging poverty is understandably financial and almost strictly fiscal, measured in what's called "absolute terms." The federal government defines the poor in America as those who make approximately $23,050 a year for a family of four.[1] The U.S. Census Bureau reports that 16 percent of the American population lives in poverty, including 20 percent of our children. And all the numbers have gotten worse in the past twenty years. In fact, between the ages of twenty-five and seventy-five, 58.4 percent of Americans will spend at least one year below the government-defined poverty line.[2]

However, the federal government's poverty statistics, accurate though they may be, do not in any way define the absolute state of the American experience of poverty. The real poverty we must battle is a state of being rather than a simple statement of financial condition. It is much more connected to aspiration, emotions, psychology, and hope than it is to financial or material analysis. Therefore, my approach reflects behavioral rather than traditional economics. I believe that we define poverty in America too narrowly. Because we don't really understand poverty, we mislabel it, disassociate ourselves from it, and then, ashamed that we have any of it at all as part of our pristine American experience, lock it away in a sort of a repressed psychological box labeled, "Not me; not us."

Discussing poverty in America today is arguably even more taboo than discussing race. At least we talk about race. We are ashamed of what we think we know and understand about poverty, and as a result, like all forms of shame, we really don't want to deal with it. And this of course makes solving it almost impossible.

My objective is to expand and deepen this definition of poverty; to dilute, redefine, reimagine, and, most important, remove the shame of this definition. To replace it with the only label we need: *hope.*

The Poor Aren't Who We Think They Are

I wish to move away from the unproductive argument surrounding poverty and toward a broader reimagining of what it means to be poor, reflecting the modern reality that is often missed in the purely statistical dialectic. To resolve this internal conflict, I recommend reframing the discussion around what we might call the "teetering class."

We often get tied up in knots over the definition of poverty as exclusively an issue of income, thinking that only low-income people are poor or suffer the consequences of poverty. This is misleading, and frankly it is meant to mislead in some instances, to reduce the discussion to an argument that can rarely be resolved. I don't wish to argue this point.

America has a teetering class of people from all walks of

life, living with a wobbling sense of staggering uncertainty. These aren't just the poor. These are the nearly poor, the almost poor, the could be poor, the was poor, the really poor, the somewhat poor, the temporarily poor, and, of course, the persistently poor. This class of Americans is hard to define. It extends across traditional class, race, and economic lines. It includes people who work and don't earn enough to cover their expenses, whether this is a low-income single mother earning a living as a waitress or a married midlevel accountant earning $50,000. They represent a diverse but interconnected, multiracial population of average, everyday American heroes and "sheroes" living all too often with too much month at the end of their money. They teeter from one paycheck to the next, from one emergency to the next, one step ahead of collection notices, late fees, overdraft fees, and utility cutoff schedules. That sense of perpetual worry gnaws at a person's psyche, and over time begins to erode one's sense of self-confidence,

This class of people keeps America strong and moving. These people are raising families in struggling households both large and small, both urban and rural, both black and white, and somehow they are finding creative ways to make ends meet and to live life with dignity. Often, they find themselves hoping against hope that all of it will simply work out on its own.

The recent economic crises pulled many more members of what we call the middle class into this new reality of the teetering class, with the accompanying disabling characteristics. "Middle class" once meant stability, whether for a blue-collar worker such as a factory worker or a white-collar worker such as a college professor. Job and income stability meant one parent could stay home to raise the children. In the current economy, many members of the formerly blue-collar middle class have fallen into poverty, leaving a contracting middle class composed of more white-collar workers but with two working parents. These parents are competing with the streets to raise their children, and after twenty years of hard work and sacrifice, many find that they are not making any more money.

Today's middle class is a tightrope, precariously perched on the precipice of financial ruin. It is unsure, unsteady, and quivering with uncertainty not only about its own future but also about the future of its children. Middle-class Americans are worried and embarrassed that, for the first time in a century, it seems as though our children's future may not be as bright as our own. This is the teetering class: anxious, insecure, stressed, overworked, and worried. This class—this psychological class—is as likely to have high incomes as low incomes, whether people are living on $75,000 in a major city or $15,000 in Des Moines, Iowa. An annual income of $50,000, which is the earning of about half of all American families, is just about the point at which living standards become tight in a city such as Washington, DC. So this condition is detached from absolute income and is more related to overall money management and long-term stability.

The emotional and psychological effects of being a part of the teetering class are many. First, it results in a lack of self-confidence and self-esteem. This is about half the problem. A person who doesn't feel good about himself or herself is screwed in America. If you don't believe in yourself, no one else will. Second, poverty results in a lack of positive role models and a crappy environment in a person's immediate community. Finally, poverty produces a lack of opportunity in education, educational quality, and educational attainment; a lack of relationship wealth, or "who you know"; and a lack of access to capital and knowledge, financial or otherwise.

A person can experience two of these disabling characteristics and survive, perhaps even feel successful, maybe even for a long time. But a person who experiences all three of them has a slim chance—or no chance—of success in America.

This shift has damaged the self-esteem and personal self-confidence of these people as well as their access to real, sustainable opportunity. Many are now among the permanently unemployed who have been without a job for six months or longer, and, in the new job market, many who once made $75,000 or $100,000 annually are settling into new job opportunities paying $40,000 to $50,000 annually. All around them, positive and aspirational role models have significantly thinned out as peers, family, and friends have also lost their jobs or changed jobs, and their immediate environment has suffered serious hits of aspiration and hope.

Add to this the increasing overall cost of living over the years, the consistent migration from rural areas to major cities, and the overall static income in America over thirty to forty years, and you have middle-class families who actually feel poor.[3]

But if individuals making $50,000 annually are struggling to make it, what are the prospects for those making $25,000 annually, with two children and the equivalent of a high school education? Considering that 76 percent of all Americans are living from paycheck to paycheck[4] and more than 60 percent of American gross domestic product is consumer driven,[5] we are effectively starving our chief economic engine—the American middle class and those aspiring to join them.

Opportunity (Not) Knocking

People meeting this new definition of poverty are as likely to be someone we know as to be someone we hear about in the news. But they all have one thing in common: they live outside the beltway of American opportunity.

Obviously, people don't wake up one morning and decide to be poor; nor do they want their children to be poor. Most parents want their children to be successful, hard-working, taxpaying citizens, both for their own good and as a matter of pride. But people can't give what they don't have. They emulate what they see around them, and what most poor people today see are others just like them, who lack financial literacy and access to banking and finance, who have poor credit scores, who may not have a job, who probably don't own a home. Their neighborhoods don't include many positive role models, entre-preneurs, or business owners. And most of all, they don't see a lot of hope.

Driving through urban, inner-city communities reveals cen-trally located real estate (usually within five miles of a city's downtown) that is either run down or looks completely aban-doned, though it is supposedly home to the poor. There are check cashers next to payday lenders next to title lenders, and rent-to-own stores next to liquor stores. This is what I call a 500 credit score community. A 500 credit score community—

like a 500 credit score individual—has a certain personality, behavior, and value set. Low credit scores tend to drag along with them low levels of hope and self-esteem, low levels of financial literacy, and low levels of education and aspiration. People in this position become easy marks for those who see poverty as something to be exploited rather than as potential to be nurtured. The existence of such communities triggers mostly one-way prosperity, with money flowing almost exclusively toward the owners of the enterprises.

The poor and working classes have always striven to get on the path to the middle-class American dream. This was a solid aspirational dream for generations of Americans from World War II forward and it worked as the ultimate stabilizer for society. Nothing stabilizes society better or faster than a good job and a shot at aspirational success. I call it the hope factor, and hope takes off like bamboo when it is planted within the ecosystem of a city environment primed for growth.

But today's poor and working classes all too often do not occupy an ecosystem of hope or an environment primed for growth. In fact, growing up in this kind of neighborhood, I learned that no matter how nice the people in a community might be, poverty is just as much a culture as success is. And the culture of poverty stretches out into just about every aspect of one's life.

The American Psychological Association reported that job pressure and stress are the top two causes of stress in America. The poor experience the greatest amount of these two kinds of stress and are therefore highly likely to be constantly experiencing finance-related stress, which can actually impede cognitive function.[6] This psychological effect can further perpetuate poverty in a debilitating cycle.

Statistically, poor people also have poor access to health care and housing. Their diet is often of poor quality—after all, fresh fruit and vegetables are expensive (and even inaccessible in some neighborhoods, known as "food deserts"), but feeding a family of four at a fast-food restaurant is cheap, accessible, and easy. And poor people, by definition, have poor financial service options. In fact, the poorest actually pay the most for their financial services. This sense of lack and financial insecurity, along with financial illiteracy, begins to bleed into the lane of opportunity, too.

The disadvantages faced by the poor go on and on. Basically, when you are poor, most everything is a challenge, and this translates into poor overall well-being. The top causes of bankruptcy are medical expenses, unemployment, and debt, accounting for 79 percent of all bankruptcies. And to complete the cycle of poverty, these weak financial conditions often make it harder to find a job, with 47 percent of U.S. employers requiring a credit report as part of the hiring process.[7]

And this, of course, is being passed down to the next generation. Poor children have poor educational attainment opportunities. Schools in poor neighborhoods tend to be run down, understaffed, and short on supplies or enrichment opportunities, but the main reason that minority kids drop out of school is not academics but money.[8] They either leave school early to make money to support their families or they drop out because they don't see that education will ever make them any money. Students drop out of college—overwhelmingly so—because of the cost of this same education. They or their families either can't afford the cost of tuition or can't afford or access student loans.

If we fail to do address these issues, we will find ourselves as a new second-tier nation, focusing all of our time, energy, and ever-decreasing resources on surviving at home rather than thriving around the world. We will become the nation that *used to* lead the world. We are all in this together.

The Rich Aren't Who We Think They Are

Just as the poor are not who we might think they are, neither are the so-called rich. The advantages they enjoy are both financial and a mirror image of the disabling characteristics I outlined in relation to the new definition of poverty. Relative to the poor, the well-off possess incredibly high levels of self-esteem and self-confidence. In fact, *this* is this group's real wealth. Second, they possess strong and positive role models, typically beginning with their parents, a strong and stable community environment, and most notably, access to vitally important business role models. Finally, this group possesses strong and natural access to opportunity in their lives—strong schools, top-flight educational access, and educational resources. They also possess a natural network of family relationships to help them navigate circles of power and influence.

People making $100,000 or more a year are not necessarily on Easy Street, but they do live on a different street in the ways that matter most. They typically hold advanced degrees, and as a result they retain the invaluable set of college relationships that continues to pay both financial and nonfinancial opportunity dividends. Their families enjoy this same informal benefit loop, from an informal e-mail that facilitates a job to an informal phone call that fast-tracks college acceptance at a highly sought institution. Fifth-generation Yale graduates don't just happen. It is intentional and is based as much on relationships and social comfort as it is on competence.

Today our major issue is not so much race, the color line, or social strife as it is class and poverty. Just when we are starting to get our hands around all the racial challenges facing America, creating institutions, organizations, and laws to deal with these injustices, here comes an entirely new form of barrier—class, wealth, and privilege. There are increasingly two worlds—the rich one, where people make $100,000 or more, and then everyone else.

It makes complete sense that the wealthy, educated, and privileged would prefer not to deal with the problems they see every day on the news and on the streets, problems that don't seem to have any solutions. All the crime, drugs, overflowing prisons, crumbling schools, and general despair are frustrating to rational adults of all races and social strata. So it's understandable that those who can afford to do so might like to retreat to gated communities and private schools, hire private security, hide out in private clubs.

Unfortunately, if we go down this path, society will fray and fall apart, because the hope within people will fall away. And if hope falls away, no private gated community or private security force will keep anyone safe. Turning off and turning away doesn't work. We cannot turn away and turn inside simply because people are difficult and our problems seem intractable.

The Wealthy Won't Stay Wealthy if We Keep the Poor Out

The irony is that the privileged class is at least in part utterly frustrated by an environment it helped to create by turning its back. When society succeeds, we all played a role in that, but when it fails, we must cop to that participation also. The rich need everyone else, if only to stay rich. Manufacturers need people to buy their products, retailers need customers for their goods, technology companies need users. And even more, the well-off must remember who works in their homes and businesses, who caters to their needs and handles the details of their lives, who takes care of and even educates their children.

The poor are all around us, and it is actually *because* of them and their belief that there is still enough hope left over for them that society still works, that cities are still civilized, that most people still stop at red lights and are law-abiding citizens. It is because of the working poor, the underserved, and the struggling middle class that America works at all. *That* America *is* America.

If the rich and privileged simply decide to disappear behind their walls, the things that they depend upon for their largess will fall away, will be torn away, or will be destroyed. This is a global problem, not unique to America, but it is a most immediate risk here in the United States because of our reliance on freedom, life, liberty, and the promise of our Constitution at the heart of the American experience.

But there is another way, rooted in a new partnership between government, community, and the private sector that focuses on actually solving our problems in a holistic way.

This is a partnership between the rich and the poor, focused not merely on decreasing problems and poverty but also on increasing levels of aspiration, hope, engagement, well-being, and, with all of that, increased economic energy and increased gross domestic product.

Eighty-four percent of all tax revenue in the state of California is paid by 15 percent of California taxpayers.[9] To me, that's not a problem, that's a new American opportunity. It means there are another 85 percent of Californians who could be contributing more, doing more, aspiring more, and adding more to California's bottom line. Immigrants or their children founded more than 40 percent of Fortune 500 companies, which collectively employ more than ten million people and today generate total annual revenues of more than $4.2 trillion.[10] Furthermore, for some time, the job growth engine in America has been small businesses, entrepreneurs, start-ups, and what is often referred to as "shoot-ups." Every big business was once a small one, and the thirty-eight million residents of California represent a huge, mostly untapped reservoir of economic energy.

The poor and the working class are not a problem to be dealt with but the keepers of an untapped opportunity that can be leveraged for the benefit of America. They are not just reliable consumers but also are future producers of economic recovery.

Economic Power Is Political Power

Governments and public spaces were not nearly the first to desegregate, or to be desegregated. It was business that did this first in the South.

Dr. King was unique and special for many reasons in addition to his brilliance as a strategic thinker, planner, and marketer. For one, he was an optimist. He figured out what he was for, when most others simply knew what they were against. Dr. King also knew how to spot a trend and then leverage and utilize the untapped strengths of those around him, including his staff and key advisors.

When Rosa Parks refused to give up her seat to a white passenger on a Montgomery, Alabama, bus on December 1, 1955, she wasn't trying to be a hero. But Ms. Parks catapulted Dr. King into the leadership of the movement for civil rights and, what was less obvious, made possible the first big a-ha moment of the movement in the period that followed. It was a silver rights moment.

Following the arrest of Parks, blacks refused to ride the buses, on the grounds that if they could not sit where they liked, they would rather not sit on the bus at all. For a time they even created their own transportation and taxi services to move the black population around the city.

Unfortunately for the bus company, most of its customers in Montgomery were black, and blacks' refusal to patronize the business eventually bankrupted it. The protesters did not initially avoid the buses in an effort to hurt the bus company, but they were not blind to the fact that when, as a group, they avoided the immoral and unethical business policies of the bus company, it really hurt.

It was a lesson in simple economics and a reminder that the black population was the simple majority—and a majority of the customers—in most of these small towns. These realizations settled in the back of the nimble mind of Dr. King as a life lesson, and after nine months this "moral plan" became a de facto business plan for the movement. Later, whenever Dr. King entered a town to march for truth, justice, and freedom, he had a few organizational rules to go along with the emotions of the plan. For instance, he forbade violence on the part of the marchers, who would preferably include a lot of well-dressed, respectable women and kids. He was also media savvy, so all marches were to be staged before 2 P.M., which would allow coverage of the march on the six o'clock evening news, in those days before the twenty-four-hour news cycle.

Most importantly, however, after weeks of marching and a general black consumer pullback from local merchants in a town, Dr. King quietly sent in his chief deputy and strategist, Andrew Young, to meet with the local business elite. The theory was simple: the freeze on consumer spending was hurting business, and if Young could get one hundred local business leaders in any of those small towns to agree to anything, the local recalcitrant political leadership would ultimately come along for the ride.

Young was never really seen leading marches, nor was he arrested, because Dr. King didn't want him to be. Young was more valuable as a calm negotiator at closed-door business meetings than as another bruised and battered civil rights warrior sitting in a jail cell.

Time and time again, the strategy worked, and thus it was the business community, not local government or public institutions such as local colleges and universities, that first desegregated the South. Think lunch counters at Woolworth's or protests against the Whites Only signs at other commercial and retail establishments throughout the South. All of that all came first, before political reform. The business community desegregated the South and then governments begrudgingly followed. Civil rights in the streets accompanied by silver rights in the suites—it took both, working in concert and within an ethical framework, for the plan to work.

Financial literacy, one kind of empowerment in the new world in which we live, is the new civil rights issue for a generation. And a new generation, empowered with the confidence that comes with knowing better in order to do better, would radically change our national economy. It also would greatly influence which industries win and which lose. Imagine a generation of educated, confident individuals, empowered with financial literacy and an increased credit score, and then reflect on how well the more than thirteen thousand nonbank, often predatory financial institutions would fare in this new world where the consumer is king.

The New American Royalty: Consumers

When Henry Ford introduced his first automobile, he was smart enough to pay his workers enough to buy the automobiles they were building. Ford's factory production approach was all about volume, and he realized there was no point in building a lot of cars if he didn't have a lot of customers. Ford's insight helped usher in the birth of the American middle class—and provided a kick start for the city of Detroit.

Since that time to today, from Detroit to Silicon Valley, it has been the masses of America, not the high-end classes of America alone, driving this economic juggernaut. In fact, with the notable exception of wealth gained through criminal activity, war, government contracting, and the like, almost all real wealth accumulation in this country has come through the working poor, the struggling classes, and a broad middle class.

A couple of decades after Ford, another automobile manufacturer learned what Ford had already shown. General Motors' Cadillac division was faltering in the 1930s. In 1928 the company manufactured 41,172 Cadillacs; by 1933 Cadillac sold only 6,736 cars, a decline of fully 84 percent. It was losing so much money that the board of directors was debating whether to close the division down entirely.[11]

Luckily for GM, it had Nicholas Dreystadt. As Dreystadt traveled around the country, calling on the service departments of Cadillac dealers, he noticed that a significant number of Cadillac owners were black, even though Cadillac, which was after the prestige market, refused to sell to blacks. These owners were buying the cars through white straw buyers.

Dreystadt encouraged the board of directors to drop its discriminatory policies and begin selling Cadillacs directly to black customers. The board bought his reasoning, and in 1934 Cadillac sales increased by 70 percent. The division actually broke even. And during still-depressed 1937, more Cadillacs were sold than during roaring 1928.

This changed the industry, but it also changed the consumer. The black consumer gained respect as a legitimate economic force multiplier that could in fact lift the economy, if not radically transform and save an entire company and countless jobs.

The clout of poor and working-class people is no less powerful today. Walmart, founded by a man who drove a pickup truck until the very day he died, was created to provide affordable and quality products to and for the working class and the working poor. Although the company has a controversial record on the treatment and fair pay of its workers, it is nonetheless the largest retailer in the world today, and one of the largest employers of minorities, women, and people of color.

But the really instructive point here is that the biggest retailer in the world is not Nordstrom or Macy's, Neiman Marcus or Barneys. It's Walmart, by a long shot. The store that serves the working class, not the stores that serve the wealthy class or even primarily the middle class, dominates the retailer landscape. Other heavyweight retailers such as Target and Costco also cater to the working-class to middle-class customer.

In the service sector, restaurants exhibit the same bottom-up support. The restaurant, when first introduced as something other than a rest stop for weary travelers, was truly a perk for the wealthy and well-to-do. Today, of course, we have restaurants inside gas stations and supermarkets. Restaurants took off and became a sustainable business model when they became commoditized in many ways for the growing working and middle classes. In addition to the billions of dollars of annual revenue generated by restaurants, of course, the industry also provides jobs and economic opportunity for small business owners and working-class employees.

Even items such as telephones owe their huge success to the massive numbers of people who want to own them. The telephone was originally only accessible to the wealthy and well heeled, but Ma Bell and the national network of shareholder-funded telecoms did not grow and prosper until the landline telephone was made available to the masses and was broadly adopted by the American working class. Then the industry exploded, original investors and business innovators got rich, and the poor and underserved got something of real value.

Today, of course, the telephone is ubiquitous, particularly in its new iteration as mobile and smart phones, and owning a phone is no longer just the dream of people in the developed world. Youth and adults in the developing world are taking up mobile phones at such a rapid rate that there are today almost more mobile phones in the world than people—more than 6 billion units.[12] When the mobile phone was first introduced it was a true perk, costing upwards of $3,000. Today, the mobile phone is so common that Africa will probably begin to phase out landlines and become the first continent to focus solely on wireless in the near future. People who don't have running water, a roof over their heads, or paved roads in front of their homes have a mobile phone.

The mobile phone industry has become one of the most profitable industries of the past hundred years, making countless entrepreneurs and shareholders immensely wealthy while increasing the connectivity and empowerment of communities and individuals the world over. And its success has been driven by the working poor, the underserved, and the struggling classes, both in the United States and around the world.

Even the humble indoor toilet, taken for granted today, was originally something only the wealthy and the privileged enjoyed universal access to. It was not until the early twentieth century that the toilet entered the American mainstream, in part because of education among the populace about its benefits but particularly because the cost radically dropped. Few things have changed the lives of the working poor, working class, and middle class in America more than the indoor toilet. This not only was a benefit for society but also created a new industry.

An Untapped, Unleveraged Asset

On and on it goes. Most recently we've seen Silicon Valley transform America as its working-class, middle-class, and immigrant entrepreneurs create companies and technologies that speak to the masses. And although we are talking about billions of downloads and micro transactions, we are not talking about small dollars. This incredible expansion of market opportunity created wealth from an idea as shareholders and entrepreneurs from countless companies grew market capitalization and shareholder value in an industry that didn't previously exist. But without financial literacy, an enabling environment that includes access to banking, credit, and good business role models, and the opportunity to act on these entrepreneurial dreams, such ideas will remain only dreams.

There is a difference between being broke and being poor. Being broke is a temporary economic condition, but being poor is a disabling frame of mind and a depressed condition of the spirit. It leads to a whole culture of tending to see the glass as half empty rather than half full, of seeing oneself as the victim rather than the victor, as a consumer rather than a producer or a manufacturer of ideas.

If people don't know better they cannot do better. Ignorance is actually worse than no knowledge at all, because ignorance sends otherwise well-meaning individuals off in strange,

often unproductive directions. And all for nothing. As someone once said, "If you hang around nine poor people, it's likely
you will be the tenth."

Whatever their color, everyone wants to see some more
green (as in U.S. currency), and this represents an opportunity. What would happen if we moved credit scores in poor
neighborhoods from an average of 500 to an average of 650 or
better? Everything would change. Check cashers and payday
lenders would turn into banks and credit unions; liquor stores
would be converted into convenience stores and grocery stores.
The more consumer empowerment a community experiences
as a deep, new character trait, the less consumer protection it
or anyone in it needs.

I believe that the poor are an untapped, unleveraged asset
for the future prosperity of our nation and that America's inner
cities are the last bastion of lost capitalism. I believe that we all
lose when we default to a fear-based leadership approach that
simply locks up and throws away the keys to unique American
assets—our youth—and our only hope for future prosperity,
without first exploring whether there are rainbows possible
after these storms. We must restore hope and get people moving again by improving their financial literacy and their credit
scores, increasing their access to banking and investment, and
increasing their self-esteem and access to positive business
and personal role models.

PART II

INVESTING IN HOPE

CHAPTER THREE

Cracking the Code of Finance

When I was growing up in the inner cities of South Central Los Angeles and Compton, I didn't have a clue about free enterprise or capitalism. How did it work? How were its winners and losers picked, and who did the picking? Most important, how could I participate? Forget about it. There was no manual for poor people. We never got the memo.

All I knew was that some folks in a world far, far away were rich and well-to-do and did as they liked, wearing suits and going in and out of high-rise buildings. Meanwhile, other folks—folks I knew in my neighborhood, folks like me— struggled to understand how these rich folks achieved any of that. There was no building above three floors in my entire neighborhood, and the only dress suit these families owned were considered Sunday best or reserved for funeral services. Most everyone who owned or ran a business or a major corporate store like Thrifty's (now replaced by the likes of CVS or Walgreens in most communities) didn't actually *live* in our neighborhood. They made their money and by sundown they were gone.

And precisely because people in my neighborhood didn't understand this thing called capitalism, we feared it. We assumed it must be evil and wrong or else why were we being excluded? No one in my neighborhood could explain it or relate to the power that came with it. For us this was in many ways a triple hit. First, we didn't understand the system or how it worked. Second, those who did understand the system only took money out of the community. Money barely circulated through our neighborhood once, with our help, and then promptly left. And finally, related to this, many business owners employed friends or members of their own families rather than the neighborhood kids. Thus, these businesses did little to create local jobs and often actually helped to feed a slow-cooking community rage.

It did not help that the local pastor often suggested that it was hard to be rich and remain close to God, and worse, that to be poor was almost a virtue. That God *loves* poor people. And although it's true that it's difficult (though not impossible) to be rich and to remain close to God, and although God does love poor people, He does not love them *because* they are poor! Rather, He loves and cares for and calls out for this group specifically because no one else seems to, because the world continuously turns its back on the poor, and because if He doesn't care for them, then who will?

Unfortunately, my pastor had missed the point of Proverbs 10:4: "He becometh poor that dealeth with a slack hand: but the hand of the diligent maketh rich." To be poor is *not* to not have anything. To be poor is to not *do anything*, and lazy hands make a man poor. God here is modeling true success behavior, arguing for industry. He is in essence saying, "Why give a man a fish? When you can, *teach* a man to fish."

During a trip that Dr. King, Andrew Young, and Coretta Scott King took to Israel, a reporter commented that Dr. King reminded him of the Good Samaritan on the Jericho Road. Dr. King never responded to this reporter, and Young wanted to know why. Dr. King's response was simple and to the point.

"Andy," he said, "I am tired of seeing my people sitting in a ditch along the side of the road, like victims. The Jericho Road is a dangerous road. . . . We must work to fix the Jericho Road, pave the Jericho Road, put streetlights up along the Jericho Road."

We need a new generation of educated and empowered young people, a new generation of financially literate, empowered homeowners and small business owners along the Jericho Road. All of this points toward industry, toward the inherent value and dignity of our own work, of creating value through that work, and of doing for oneself when possible. But first we must banish ignorance and replace it with knowledge. I call such knowledge capital financial literacy, and from it rises hope.

The neighborhood where I grew up included some of the nicest, kindest, most decent people in the world, but with respect to unlocking the miracles of free enterprise, capitalism, entrepreneurship, job or wealth creation in and for the community, it was the blind leading the blind. What we didn't know that we didn't know was killing us, even though we *thought* we knew this. I just kept running into the same reality: the outsiders operating in my community knew something different from the insiders who actually called my community home.

The Global Language of Money

Financial literacy is nothing less than the new global language of money, and in today's world we all need to be bilingual. Yet we as a nation are failing to teach our poor people to fish. We are failing to provide them with financial literacy. Most poor people in the world today have no idea what successful people are talking about. Asking poor people to read *The Wall Street Journal* is about like asking them to read and speak advanced Russian.

Unfortunately, harnessing the economic energy of the poor and underserved is not part of the success formula for the United States in the twenty-first century, and this is one reason why many citizens of this great nation of ours find themselves poor and underserved. But it was not always that way.

President Lincoln, one of the original visionaries for the nation, had a vision of winning the Civil War, but he also envisioned freeing the enslaved and ensuring their future economic prosperity. Not long after he signed the Emancipation Proclamation, he signed legislation creating the Freedman's Saving and Trust Company, commonly known as the Freedman's Savings Bank. The president considered the bank's mission so important to the nation that its offices were eventually located directly across from the U.S. Department of the Treasury, perpendicular to the White House, where the president could see it and keep his eye on it.

The bank's mission was radical—to teach newly freed black Americans about money. That's nineteenth-century government-sanctioned financial literacy education in action. In addition to helping blacks build up savings and gain financial literacy, the bank also enabled community organizations to prosper and expand. Unfortunately, bank speculation dashed the hopes and dreams of more than seventy thousand poor black depositors, mostly sharecroppers in an agrarian age, and by the late 1800s even the great Frederick Douglass, the last president of the bank, could not save the bank.

One hundred thirty years later we have an entire group of people—more than thirty million African-Americans alone—who have never been given a lesson in the global language of money or how the free enterprise system or capitalism works. They have not been given financial literacy. The black middle class didn't emerge until nearly a century later, following World War II, when black workers finally got new access to government jobs and careers in various fields.

These people are not stupid; they are simply limited in their financial literacy. Today, the net worth of middle-class blacks is a fraction of the net worth of their white counterparts,[1] who have simply had better financial and economic role models for a much longer time. They have experienced embedded lessons in financial literacy, free enterprise, and capitalism as the world practices it. And when you know better, you tend to do better.

But this is not exclusively or even mostly a black and brown problem. There are more poor whites in America today than poor anybody else. Dr. King, inspired by a young Marian Wright Edelman (founder of the Children's Defense Fund), called forth his final movement in 1968 with the Poor People's Campaign, which was inclusive of all races, cultures, and creeds, because he knew that we are all in this together.

Today, entire swatches of communities and cities are populated with the poor, who do not make any discernible economic contribution to the nation. Unfortunately, in fact, they cost us money. Even worse, however, is that they have no clue they are even laboring in a sea of economic ignorance. In short, it's not what they don't know that's killing them; it's what they think they know.

Rainbows after Storms

You cannot have a rainbow without first experiencing a storm. And America's so-called poor neighborhoods and communities have weathered plenty of storms. These once were dynamic, successful economies, and if you count today's underground cash economy, these neighborhoods are still generating tremendous off-the-books economic activity. According to Social Compact, inner-city communities are larger, safer, and have far greater buying power than is indicated by standard market information sources. The most downtrodden of these so-called poor neighborhoods also have baseline American infrastructure and enjoy the rule of law in the most progressive market economy in the world. Most important, these communities have an enormous unmet need for mainstream banking services; access to credit; access to real estate investment and home ownership; and income generation through small businesses such as gas stations, convenience stores, grocery stores, and entertainment. But before they can create these things that every community needs, before they can find their way out of the storm to see that rainbow, the people living there must achieve financial literacy.

When I was nine or ten years old, I was lucky enough to be

enrolled in what seemed like the last financial literacy class broadly offered in public schools: Home Economics. I just loved that class, could not wait to go, because it was practical and it connected what I was learning in school with how I soon needed to be living.

One day a banker came into our classroom to teach a financial literacy lesson. The banker was white but he might as well have been orange. He wasn't from a different race; he was from a different planet—that place where rich folks lived, which I saw so often on television. He was wearing a blue suit, a red tie, and a white shirt and he was speaking a different language from all of us, the language of money.

I decided I was going to become fluent in this language. About halfway through this class, I asked him, completely seriously, "Sir, how did you get rich, legally?" I asked him what he did and who he financed, where he lived and what he drove. I just couldn't process any of this. But I remember that this caught me cold: he said he financed entrepreneurs. Whatever *that* was, I decided, I wanted to be one!

I didn't even know what the phrase "financial literacy" meant back then, but I know it changed my life. In the banker's responses to my questions I got a glimpse at the memo that my community had not yet received. I became passionate about entrepreneurship because of that experience. I teach financial literacy to young people today because of that experience. I wear business suits today because of that experience—along with watching my father wear suits two or three times every week.

If that one visit from the banker to my classroom had such a profound effect on my life, imagine the changes that could come about if we endowed everyone with the transformational power of financial literacy and the internal wealth of human dignity.

Defining Financial Literacy in a New Economic Age

The poor must become bilingual, must learn the language of money. Financial literacy has evolved over time, and thankfully it continues to evolve. In moving forward, it is helpful to keep in mind an insightful quote from the founder of LinkedIn: "If you are not slightly embarrassed by your 1.0 software release, then you released too late."[2] It is better to do something good today than to wait for whatever you view or feel to be perfect sometime later. Action is paramount in today's day and age.

Financial education is the baseline, pioneered for under-served Americans through President Lincoln's creation of the Freedman's Savings Bank and for mainstream Americans through organizations such as Junior Achievement, about one hundred years ago. Junior Achievement was created to help young people in rural America prepare themselves to run and operate their family farms. For these young people, the issues were not based on emotion or self-esteem but on fundamentals, and this mainstream community program was tied to private family wealth protection and wealth creation.

Today, however, issues of money and the economy are mixed up and interrelated with emotions, self-esteem, identity, even core issues of human dignity, particularly in inner-city and underserved America. Thus, my founding of Operation HOPE more than twenty years ago to address this need focused on the one hundred million Americans who make $50,000 or less, who define themselves as the working poor or the under-served. Today, this also includes the struggling middle class. These people, families, small businesses, and communities need to speak the language of financial literacy to help turn their situation around.

This language includes several elements, all of which are important. We have been discussing **financial literacy**, which represents the basic and essential tools in the financial educa-tion tool kit. **Financial capability** represents both the potential and the absolute awareness of what is possible, one's options and opportunities, after one has achieved financial educa-tion and financial literacy. **Financial inclusion** represents the vision and commitment of America to include everyone in its future promise and opportunity. **Financial empowerment** is what one does with one's newly discovered financial capability. And **financial dignity** is the goal of all financial empowerment efforts, just as the civil rights movement was really a campaign for respect and dignity.

Following the recent global economic crises, an entire gen-eration of young people is on the cusp of some of the most important decisions of their lifetimes, and it is our responsibil-ity to give them the tools they need to become the new individ-ual and community assets of economic energy that America needs to rediscover its greatness and create a new generation of sustainable jobs for all.

Financial Literacy Is a Bottom-Up Solution

Financial literacy is not just about the individual, however. As Lincoln understood, producing capable financial citizens is also good public policy. Governments are increasingly broke, and they should not be the principal creators of jobs. The first $700 billion stimulus package, tied to the global economic crisis affecting the United States, was substantially about filling holes in county and state budgets. This was an adequate response to the immediacy of the crisis but it is not a long-term answer. States need the same thing that poor folks need, more (new) jobs and more revenue, and this begins with more financial literacy.

For instance, a substantial driver of county and state income is related to property tax revenue, and the crisis that sparked this larger global economic crisis (now a crisis of confidence) was a predatory subprime mortgage crisis. As we have subsequently learned, a good deal of the blame for this crisis falls on the shoulders of predatory subprime lenders trading in greed, fraud, and the like. However, an important partner in the crisis included otherwise well-educated borrowers who, when obtaining a loan, asked "What's the payment?" and not "What's the interest rate?" And as anyone schooled in financial literacy knows, one should never focus solely on the payment—it's the interest rate that is important. Unfortunately, a similarly predatory subprime lender got my father twenty years ago, but they never got me because I made sure I was financially literate, that I spoke the language of money in an economic age.

We must give everyone those same tools. We must make financial literacy—teaching each and every one of our children the language of money—the new civil rights issue for twenty-first century America. As Andrew Young told me, "Dr. King and I integrated the lunch counter, but we never integrated the dollar. And to live in a system of free enterprise and yet not to understand the rules of free enterprise is the definition of slavery." To not understand the language of money today is to be an economic slave.

What our poor communities need are not just campaigns against social injustice but campaigns that promote economic justice and real opportunity. Consider, for example, the benefit of educating people about the Earned Income Tax Credit. Approximately one in four Americans who qualify for this earned cash reward for working people, written into the federal tax code, never even ask for it. We're talking about $9 billion to $10 billion annually that goes unclaimed by people who could really use it to pay a mortgage, pay off a car, fund an education, or otherwise reduce family financial pressure. Ten billion dollars injected into poor and underserved neighborhoods throughout America—$30 billion to $50 billion over a three- to five-year period—holds real transformational promise not only for the so-called poor but also for America itself. But people must be informed about their right to access this money in order to benefit from it.

A Missed Opportunity

During the final period of the Civil War, one of Lincoln's top generals promised all freed slaves forty acres and a mule, an opportunity to own collateral and machinery in their own names. It wasn't Lincoln's idea or his official policy, though he was supportive of the initiative. As we have seen, however, Lincoln did sign the Freedman's Bureau Act of 1865, which among other things created the Freedman's Savings Bank.

Unfortunately, Lincoln was killed less than thirty days after signing this new act, and President Andrew Johnson, who filled Lincoln's vacated office, had diametrically opposed views on things like the Freedman's Savings Bank. Johnson was what today we would call a hard-core Southern segregationist, and he was quoted as saying, "As long as I am President, this nation will be white run."[3] So much for all of Lincoln's black empowerment ideas.

Because he could not easily kill the bank, Johnson decided to simply ignore and defund it, and he essentially told Southern lawmakers to ignore federal law—a precedent that ultimately morphed into Jim Crow laws in the Southern states. But good and right-minded ideas are hard to kill, even when you are trying, and Lincoln's plan took a lot to kill. At its height, the Freedman's Savings Bank had seventy thousand depositors, all of whom were formerly enslaved. By placing all of the little they had in this new federal bank, these people were making the most powerful aspirational statement possible. They wanted to back their own lives and they hoped to contribute to the American experiment, no matter how they were treated. When they were given an informed choice they didn't want a handout, only a hand up.

Unfortunately, due in large part to the destructive efforts of Johnson and the mismanagement and gaming of the bank that followed, the bank ultimately did fail, and every depositor lost his or her money. All of it. This may be part of the reason that black Americans and other disadvantaged groups do not trust banks and the government today.

But what would have happened if Lincoln had survived his second term? What would America be like today if former slaves, who essentially built America for free during the agricultural age, were given and empowered with the 1865 version of collateral and machinery, financial literacy, an understanding of the language of money and the workings of the free enterprise system and capitalism, access to capital, and with it, enhanced opportunity and jobs? We simply would not have what some want to call a permanent underclass today. America would be better, stronger, and even more prosperous.

It's time to finish what Lincoln started and Dr. King never had the opportunity to meaningfully address. But this time we can and will use the power of the private sector and the free enterprise system itself, supported strongly by government, to transform people's lives. We must enable people to contribute to the American dream, to help America win again, with all of its people's shoulders against the wheel of change.

CHAPTER FOUR

Banking and Financial Services

A large goal of empowering people with financial literacy is to teach them how the banking system works and how to access it. Banking today is largely dominated by a few large players, most of which are focused on clients with resources already on hand. It's an understandable strategy, but it's limited by the same parameters that make it attractive: its known and preestablished nature. Today there are banks on almost every corner of mainstream upper- and upper-middle-class neighborhoods, essentially trading known customers back and forth. What I am proposing is new customer acquisition. Some major banks are involved in legitimate financial literacy efforts, a few of them very substantively, but much more needs to be done. This activity cannot simply be viewed as part of public relations or even of public and government affairs. It must be viewed as what it is: the lifeblood of any business or industry with the word *financial* in its name. This is nothing less than enlightened self-interest.

As it stands right now, the big banks are not really all that interested in opening accounts for poor people, but this will change just as soon as they stop seeing an emerging market as a poor market. The irony of all of this, interestingly enough, is that banking actually originated with the people, and many of today's largest banks began by serving the working poor, the working class, and the struggling middle class.

Amadeo Giannini, the son of Italian immigrants, started the Bank of Italy in a converted San Francisco saloon on October 17, 1904, with twenty-eight deposits totaling $8,780.[1] The bank was established to serve working-class citizens, especially Italian Americans living in San Francisco's North Beach neighborhood. Word about his service spread quickly, and by 1916 Giannini's bank boasted several branches in other neighborhoods. In 1928, Giannini changed the name to Bank of America and remained the bank's chairman until his death, building his little enterprise into what was once the country's largest commercial bank.

Like Lincoln's Freedman's Savings Bank, with its focus on improving the equity and financial literacy of an underserved population, Giannini "opposed the aristocratic notion of banking, with its formality, conservative policies, and high interest rates [and] established the Bank of Italy on a democratic basis. There the little fellow was welcomed and respected, given the same service as the big fellow, and granted financial aid on easy terms."[2]

Good Selfishness and Bad Selfishness

Giannini's bank served the little fellow in the community and as a result was wildly successful. It survived both the San Francisco earthquake and fire of 1906—incidentally becoming one of the first banks to offer business loans to help rebuild the city—as well as the 1929 stock market crash. And he did it all while providing his community with a much-needed service. But Giannini was probably motivated by more than just altruism; he undoubtedly wanted to make money himself, and that's fine. He was practicing what I call "good selfishness," in which one person benefits but everyone else benefits more. Raising a child, running a socially responsible business, or working for a nonprofit organization all are examples of good selfishness.

Bad selfishness, on the other hand, is where one person benefits but everyone else pays a price for it. Drug dealing is an example of bad selfishness. Good selfishness is about *we*, whereas bad selfishness is always about *me*—what do I get and when do I get it? Bad selfishness led us into the housing bubble and the mortgage crisis. Bad selfishness led companies to use complex financial instruments such as derivatives trading to gamble with other people's money. But this does not need to be the view of the financial services industry. Instead, this is a moment of opportunity. Rainbows always follow storms.

The Alternative Financial Services Industry

All too often, the alternative financial services industry has stepped in to fill the need for community financial services that are no longer available from the big banks, in the form of payday loan outfits, check cashing services, and the like. To poor communities, where financial literacy is low and financial need is high, these organizations may look like traditional banks—after all, they perform many of the same functions as a bank. But in fact many of these companies operate with entirely different objectives, often capitalizing on the poor financial literacy and scant resources of their "clients."

The alternative financial services industry in the United States is conservatively estimated to be worth well over $321 billion annually. In addition to the $58 billion check cashing business, there are buy-here-pay-here auto loan businesses ($80 billion), payday loans ($48 billion), remittances ($46 billion), open loop prepaid cards ($39 billion), refund anticipation loans ($26 billion), money orders ($17 billion), and rent-to-own transactions ($7 billion).[3]

Unfortunately, far too many of today's alternative financial services providers fall into essentially the same camp of bad selfishness that was practiced during the Jim Crow era in the South. But when an industry has annual revenues of $321 billion, you'd better believe that those benefiting will protect their interests at all costs, so the approach of this more modern group is a bit more sophisticated—or so they'd like to think. They may not act in any overtly racist manner or in any way that screams intentional discrimination. They may dispatch low-level community liaison officers to calm the nerves of those who might otherwise protest a bit too loudly. And they attach themselves to military base entrances and small, depressed rural towns with crumbling industries and decreasing job prospects just as quickly as they attach themselves to inner-city and poor urban neighborhoods filled with minorities. Their victim could be white or black as long as their payoff is green.

Even the location of these businesses is telling. It's no accident that they are typically clustered together, often on the same street or within a block of each other—and typically in the vicinity of a liquor store. It's not that they're owned by the same people (usually), but they are all feeding on the same despair. These businesses are not rooted in love or hate—they don't even care enough to hate the users of their services. Their customers' behavior, actions, and reactions don't matter to them one way or the other as long as they get paid. In fact, they don't even care enough to get their business model right. Their primary interest lies in getting rich, not in building wealth. They would rather have a successful series of transactions than build a sustainable relationship with their customers or community.

As the mortgage crisis revealed, however, the oppressive nature of the alternative financial services sector will at some point reach a negative tipping point. This model of sustained oppression is simply not sustainable at scale. It may be possible for an industry to risk destroying its customer base instead of building it up when it is targeting a small segment of our society and economy, but the unethical practices associated with some alternative financial service providers are increasingly expanding from merely the working poor. We now see these practices seeping into and even becoming common in the lives of the working class and the struggling middle class as well.

A $321 billion industry is real money, and the size of this market confirms not only that ignorance pays but also that traditional banks are in a promising position to step in and offer these consumers bank accounts and some financial literacy training, as we have recently seen done by Bank of America and Khan Academy.[4] This is a chance for banks to do well by doing good.

According to the Federal Deposit Insurance Corporation, there were forty million underbanked households in America as of 2012.[5] That's forty million customers who could be better served by a good relationship with a bank they can trust and that provides them with timely access to information. This is a moment of opportunity for the banking industry and a chance for the underserved and underbanked to have their financial capability increased. Were traditional banks to couple a no-minimum, no-hidden-fee checking account with a financial literacy course, perhaps available online, they would gain new, valuable customers while also improving the financial lives of those account holders.

Improving Banking

The increasing dilemma of the working poor and struggling middle class—faced with a baseline of financial illiteracy, ever-decreasing choices from mainstream financial institutions, and increasing encroachment of the alternative financial service sector—represents both a problem for American families in the short term and an opportunity for mainstream banking over the long term. Customers of alternative financial service providers walked away from, were turned away from, or never were customers of mainstream banks in the first place. Whatever the case, this spells opportunity for the banks willing to return to their roots in, of, and for a community.

It may be surprising to learn, however, that some alternative financial services providers can actually represent the beginnings of a bottom-up solution. For example, the *New York Times* reported on La Familia Pawn and Jewelry in Orlando, Florida, which offers check-cashing and bill-paying services in addition to access to a credit card. Although these services are offered by a pawnshop—part of an industry that has something of a reputation for taking advantage of customers in financial need—it nonetheless represents a potential option for those without access to traditional financial services. Some other pawnshops have begun offering similar services.[6]

There are some possible drawbacks to this approach, such as potentially high interest rates and a high cost for basic financial transactions compared to a traditional checking or savings account. Pawnshop banking also hampers customers' ability to build a traditional credit history. But if it is approached ethically and with appropriate oversight, the business model itself is not a problem. There is both a need as well as a reasonable place for most of these services to situate themselves in the broader marketplace.

I have actually done business (through Operation HOPE) with what I would call an ethical check casher, Nix Financial in Los Angeles. As I often say, intent does matter, and Tom Nix, the owner of Nix Financial, is a man cut from a different cloth.

Tom's father was a grocer who had done well with a small chain of neighborhood family stores, and he had a practice of cashing what he called "convenience checks" for regular customers. He always found his regular customers to be honorable people who honored their debts, and for many he even ran a tab for groceries they could not afford to pay for in a particular week. They always came back within a week or two, when they got their next paycheck, and make good on their obligation. Tom's dad never charged his customers extra for this convenience. He was glad to have their business, often over a customer's lifetime, and he made a good living.

Eventually, Tom's father found that he was cashing more and more checks, and when he added a modest 1 percent to 3 percent fee, he found he was making almost as much money cashing checks as he was selling groceries—without having to carry inventory. In time, Nix Financial was a reality, with more than thirty-five successful locations throughout South Los Angeles.

But this business model was different. Nix was involved with its community, sponsoring local league teams, passing out turkeys on Thanksgiving, giving back. The community loved the Nix family and the Nix family loved the community. The company showed this both through intent (how they ran the business) and actions (how they treated customers, employees, and the community). All of Nix's employees came from the communities it served, and Nix promoted entirely from within. Nix gave in equal measure to what it got, and this commitment continued to pay dividends in the form of a highly successful business—a solid, respected brand. And Nix did all of this while charging between 1 percent and 3 percent to cash checks, whereas the competition charged upwards of 5 percent to cash the exact same checks.

Sometime in 2000 I was approached by the vice chairman of one of the largest banks in the nation, Union Bank of California, with a novel idea. The bank wanted to significantly expand its reach and footprint in the low-wealth communities of Los Angeles but didn't want to build branches. Instead, the bank found an ethical check cashing operator (guess who?) and cut a deal with him. In the end, everybody won. Tom Nix and his family were able to trade privately held stock in their company for publicly traded stock in Union Bank. Meanwhile, Union Bank had a plug-and-play entry into the market—a community it genuinely wanted to better serve—acquiring new, ready-made customers and stepping into new locations, all at a fraction of the cost of building its own traditional bank branches.

Ultimately, the bank involved Operation HOPE as a full partner in the acquisition of Nix, giving it the role of counseling and helping to transition traditional Nix Financial customers into new Union Bank customers. When customers came in to cash a check, the tellers encouraged him or her to open a bank account, and if the customer did so, the bank would cash the check for free. It worked like a charm, involving many previously unbanked people in the banking system in the process.

At the time, it was unheard of for any major banking institution to partner with a nonprofit, let alone to provide that nonprofit with equity in the deal. Unfortunately, due to a change in federal regulations, the Nix/Union Bank/Operation HOPE model eventually had to be unwound. But Union Bank continued on as a better, more community-oriented, and even more profitable bank, and Nix was eventually approached and acquired by one of the largest credit unions in the nation. The two businesses had obviously reached the same conclusion: doing well while doing good is simply good and smart business. And it serves the community.

CHAPTER FIVE

The Working Family's Hedge Fund

Since the founding of America, real estate has always been the working family's hedge fund—a hedge against being dead broke at the end of a life of hard work. Real estate has been an absolute savior for the poor, and responsible subprime lending has done more to lift poor people out of poverty than anything else over the past fifty years. The equity these families built up funded college educations and provided collateral and start-up capital for small businesses, which are in turn the job fuel for cities and America.

The recent crisis of irresponsible, fraudulent, and speculative subprime lending did irreparable damage to these families' hedge funds, but the crisis wasn't the fault of so-called ignorant poor people. Because upper-class or wealthy neighborhoods have more than enough banks, banks often are simply trading the same customers back and forth. Oddly enough, therefore, the global subprime mortgage crisis was in some ways caused by shortsighted capitalists trying to create or manufacture clients. They did this by taking many wholly appropriate financial products and pawning them off on some innocent and possibly financially illiterate consumers who thought they were getting the deal of the century.

And although we may have heard that the poor and government community reinvestment act statutes cratered our economy, the subprime mortgage crisis was in fact a middle-class crisis. In terms of their portion of the overall mortgage market, white middle-class families took up more subprime loans than all minority groups combined, which make up less than 25 percent of the market.

Outside of irresponsible institutional lending, the single most significant factor in the subprime mortgage mess was not poverty, location, or race but single-paycheck households. When the single breadwinner in these households lost his or her job, everything behind that lost check quickly went too—retirement savings, cars, and homes.

When an individual or a family loses a home, city government loses a property tax–paying client of the municipality, and lost revenue for a city translates into fewer public services for that city, decreased public safety, and less quality education. As a result, crime increases, jobs disappear, and voter participation declines because people who don't own much tend not to vote much, either. Land values plunge and property tax revenues decrease even further. Middle-class families looking for stability, public safety, and good schools flee, and the poor—who can afford the least—end up paying the most (for financial services, among other things).

Predators win, generational prosperity is held hostage to a stifling lack of opportunity, the poor are trapped in an airtight room of financial and economic ignorance, and in time, lower levels of hope and the stench of poverty are locked in. Enough of this and a city will find itself in big trouble, as Detroit has. By July 2013, seven hundred thousand Detroit residents were living in a city with $18 billion of debt and a blighted urban center with high crime.[1] We can't allow this to happen to more cities, because as our cities go, so goes the country.

These cities were already in trouble before the financial crises hit, for a variety of reasons. But one result of the mortgage crisis was that the second economic stimulus didn't go toward building new roads and bridges, which in turn helps to create real economic stimulus, jobs, and increased gross domestic product. Instead, most of that money went toward plugging holes in city and state budgets, to make up for lost property tax revenue.

Once again, then, we see that it is not the rich and the pedigreed that drive economic growth, stabilize communities, or create sustainable gross domestic product—it is the least of God's children, going about their daily lives en masse. Poor people didn't create the crisis but the poor got blamed for it, and now they cannot get loans to become homeowners—even the *possibility* of that once-reliable hedge fund has been taken away from them.

But there is a blowback effect here as well. Even middle-class folks today cannot get a mortgage—unless, of course, they have an 800 credit score and a 30 percent down payment.[2] The markets and our government have overcorrected and now everyone seeks to avoid future mistakes by making no decisions. This is not an answer; it's capitulation, rooted in fear.

A Potential Gold Mine

But there is another way. Where most people see poor neighborhoods and discarded people, I see emerging markets, entrepreneurs, small business owners, investment growth, and job creation waiting to happen. The irony is that while poor families and communities are suffering from the effects of the subprime mortgage crisis and all of the negative effects on their communities, inner-city real estate is a potential gold mine. These communities often are fifteen minutes or less from downtown, fifteen to thirty minutes away from ports and major transportation and distribution hubs. Chicago's entire South Side fronts Lake Michigan, and in the case of Los Angeles, poor communities like the one I grew up in even have easy access to beaches!

These previously majority white communities, which turned black and brown in time, are now quietly becoming majority white again. This is not racism but pure, opportunity-driven capitalism. Unfortunately, it also only builds one-way streets of economic prosperity, mostly leading from the poor and landless to the rich and landowning. When we do this, everyone loses.

Some would say that banks are wise to avoid the potential risk of taking on a low-income earner for a loan or other financial instrument, but increasing the financial capability of the poor requires reimagining the way we measure risk. Thick file underwriting and documented character lending can improve a person's credit score and his or her ability to get a loan. Thick file underwriting documents bills, insurance payments, rent payments, local lending accounts, and other forms of credit that do not show up on a consumer credit report. Thick file underwriting is also about challenging items on a report that may be in error and adding documentation that underscores and reinforces a borrower's credibility and creditworthiness.

The bottom line here is that the poor have the power to transform their own communities; we just have to reimagine how we measure risk.

The Dignity Mortgage

As we've seen in the examples of La Familia Pawn and Jewelry and Nix Financial, nontraditional banking services do not have to be predatory or destructive but instead can help a community and can thus be constructive. Likewise, there are opportunities in the mortgage industry to appropriately use products that might otherwise be viewed as predatory, but once again, mutually beneficial implementation takes real work and care.

Negatively amortizing loans, for example, were very popular during the subprime mortgage boom. This mortgage can be appropriate for some, but it also has a potentially devastating feature: the mortgage balance increases with every payment because the borrower is only paying interest, and in fact is actually paying *less* interest than normally would be calculated for that pay period. In exchange, the borrower owes the lender a lump sum payment, due at some future date. This kind of mortgage is perfect for someone with a high net worth, good cash flow, and a tax professional running sophisticated numbers on a spreadsheet. On the other hand, this kind of mortgage is a financial and family disaster for a worker making $42,000 a year with little income flexibility.

Following the economic crises, our response cannot be to do nothing. We must do something to enable families to access home loans and get back their lost hedge funds.

In October 2012, my friend Robert Gnaizda, former general

counsel of the Greenlining Institute, and I outlined a new, sustainable, responsible, less-than-prime mortgage that we called a dignity mortgage. Our simple proposal presents very little risk, if carried out carefully, and is likely to have extraordinary support both from the vast number of Americans who dream of owning a home and from virtually all 7,300 federally insured financial institutions.

Under this plan, up to 20 percent of all home mortgages per year for three years (approximately one million mortgages per year) would be defined as dignity mortgages. Such mortgages would only be available to potential homeowners who complete prescribed comprehensive financial literacy and credit counseling programs, and Housing and Urban Development–approved home counseling organizations or the equivalent would have to certify that the potential homeowner is in a position to meet their mortgage payments even in the case of a temporary illness or loss of a job. To minimize the impact of such a temporary crisis, homeowners with an established record of prompt payments would be eligible for a brief period of deferred payments during an emergency, thereby avoiding many of the temporary payment problems that cause such havoc during recessions.

The loan approval process also would ensure that borrowers are eligible only for the homes they need, rather than for far more expensive homes—a big reason that many people found themselves in trouble when the housing market went south. Additionally, the mortgages would only be available for homes at or below 95 percent of the median price in the region, and only homeowners with an income at or below 120 percent of the regional median would be eligible.

To adjust for any additional risks (and there may not be any substantial ones), lenders would be allowed to charge up to 1.25 percentage points above the lowest prime rate for a thirty-year fixed-rate mortgage. However, this additional charge would be limited to a few years, unless the borrower failed to make timely payments, after which the rate would be adjusted downward to the fixed rate that prevailed at the time of origination and the 1.25-point premium would be applied to the borrower's principal.

Government and the banking industry should study the additional risks of such mortgages to the banks, but it is likely that within a few years it would be clear that there are few or no additional risks in lending to many of the potential homebuyers who presently are excluded. Thus, Fannie Mae and Freddie Mac, which purchase approximately 90 percent of all home loans, would be required to purchase these loans, and the loans would be treated as qualified mortgages under the Dodd–Frank Act. After this program has proven its success, it could be expanded to all low- to moderate-income families and/or to all families at up to 150 percent of median income who purchase homes at 120 percent or below the median price in the region.[3]

Dignity mortgages are only one potential solution to this crisis, but it is clear that we need some kind of solution to help people achieve the dream of home ownership. Doing nothing not only limits America's ability to recover economically (because real estate cannot truly recover unless the mortgage market recovers) but also relegates America's working class and struggling middle class to alternative financial services and private, high-cost lending sources.

The mortgage crisis will abate and mainstream interests and investors will flow back into the less-than-prime mortgage market, which is ongoing, increasing, and serves an insatiable need. The only question is whether what comes next actually lifts all boats in America or represents yet another example of some getting rich while the majority are increasingly impoverished.

PART III

NURTURING HOPE

CHAPTER SIX

700 Credit Score Communities

We have seen that in the half century since the civil rights movement and Dr. King's dream, one problem (racism) has been replaced or at least matched by another—class and poverty. This is a problem that cuts across the color line and that affects urban and rural communities alike.

We've also seen what these 500 credit score communities look like in urban areas. Call it Misery Row: those predatory check cashers next to rent-to-own stores next to payday lenders next to liquor stores. One group takes advantage of a person's financial problems and misfortune while another group benefits by helping them to forget they actually have any financial problems.

But there is something we can do to change the landscape of blight in our underserved urban and rural communities: we can improve the credit scores of the people who live there. Although credit score requirements depend on the particular lender, most people with a "good" credit score of between 650 and 750 will qualify for a loan at the most preferred rates. Scores in the 500s and low 600s, on the other hand, put borrowers in the worst risk category, from a lender's perspective.

Moving a person's credit score from 500 to 670 or even to

700 increases his or her hopefulness, aspiration, and expectations. He or she no longer needs to be victimized by unscrupulous lenders. He or she will feel more empowered and less hopeless and therefore less likely to need the escape that the liquor store seems to offer. And ultimately, over time, payday lenders, unscrupulous check cashers, and title lenders are converted into credit unions and banks. Liquor stores become convenience stores and supermarkets.

Consumer protection is vitally important to a nation, and I wholly support my friend Richard Cordray and the work being done by the Consumer Financial Protection Bureau. However, when people are making the most critical decisions of their lives, such as taking out a thirty-year mortgage, there will be no mortgage police at the kitchen table with them. There are no auto loan police standing by when they show up with great enthusiasm to the used car auto dealership, only to be greeted with the enthusiastic approval of a loan carrying an 18 percent effective interest rate.

Effective consumer protection is important, but it must be matched with consumer empowerment in underserved neighborhoods and communities. This is something beyond mere financial literacy, with an endgame that sounds and feels more like financial dignity. In fact, if we provide protection without empowerment, these communities could eventually face an option that is actually worse than highly visible yet predatory commercial lenders: no lenders at all.

This is where credit scores come in. When a person moves his or her credit score from 550 (on average) to 670 or more, everything in that person's life changes. Understanding credit scores and how to maintain them is an element of financial literacy, and when we inject the power of financial literacy into the life and mind of an individual, his or her sense of well-being and hope goes through the roof. Her engagement in her own life rises to a new level, matching her new financial skill set. Nothing about that person will ever be the same again, and changing an individual is the first step toward changing a community.

The Magic of Credit Scores

A decade ago a young man named Ryan Taylor walked into one of our Operation HOPE Banking Center offices in South Los Angeles with a vision of becoming a clothing designer. He didn't want talk; he just wanted a loan for $10,000 to get to Las Vegas for a clothing and fashion conference. In his opinion, *capital* simply meant money, and he had heard on the street that we had access to some.

We tried to explain that there is more to business than getting access to money, and that money (cash in one's pocket right now) is different from finance (money one pays to borrow). We tried to explain that one should never finance long-term equity with short-term debt because small businesses need time, patience, investment, reinvestment, and flexibility to grow, whereas bank loans are due every thirty days. We tried to explain that the word *capital* comes from the Latin word *capitalis,* or "of the head."

But Taylor ignored us almost completely. He just wanted an application. So we processed his application. After all, it's a free country, and we were providing this African-American entrepreneur with access to capital.

The story ended predictably. Our young entrepreneur returned from Las Vegas empty-handed—no cash and no orders either. The producers of the conference had done what they were trained to do best: selling others on the value of coming to their venue and then emptying participants' wallets before the event concluded.

When Taylor returned to our office he was a completely different person. He was humble, receptive, open, and hungry for knowledge about how to win. Sadly, he also now owed $10,000 to Union Bank. This time, Taylor saw the sense in our advice and he took it. He enrolled in our small business and entrepreneurship training program as well as our credit counseling program, and eighteen months later young Taylor was a new man.

Creating 700 Credit Score Communities

Following our interaction with him, Ryan Taylor committed to repaying the $10,000 loan he had previously taken out, and he simultaneously applied for a new one, also through Operation HOPE, for $35,000. This new loan represented the budgeted start-up capital for his new clothing business, DROBE. And for all those who say mainstream banks never do anything good for minorities or minority communities, this serves as a source of inspiration. Union Bank made that first loan for $10,000, really on faith, and then made a second loan of $35,000 based on a solid business plan.

In the end, both loans were repaid in full and DROBE is today a decade-old small business that is adding to the American whole. They make my suits. And Taylor himself became what America needs most: a taxpayer who is raising his children, employing people, and directly contributing to the prosperity of Los Angeles and the nation.

But Taylor, with his partner Carrie Taylor and the DROBE team, went even further. They innovated a nonprofit called LEAP, which today provides after-school programming in several inner-city schools. We helped Taylor to raise his credit score, create DROBE, and become a legitimate businessman, and today DROBE is still paying it forward. Taylor has raised the roof of aspiration not only in his own life but also for his family, his new employees, the kids in the schools where his nonprofit operates, and countless others associated with each of these units of economic energy.

Now imagine doing this same thing not just with an individual but with an entire community. With this type of empowering intervention, simply helping to raise the credit scores of individuals and families in a community, the community and culture of that community eventually changes too, all through the power of market forces and the market economy.

At Operation HOPE, for instance, we help clients to investigate their credit histories, uncover settlements that aren't reflected in their credit assessments, and dispute errors in their records. This alone moves credit scores a great deal. We also couple this with free financial literacy training so that clients better understand how to increase their own financial capability. The overwhelming majority of people, when given this basic education—the ability to navigate the financial landscape and manage credit scores—do not default on the loans or credit they are given.

We encourage banks to take similar steps to create better borrowers, which also will enable banks to become more rooted in their communities and more customer oriented. Customers of alternative financial service providers often have been repelled by banks' overdraft charges and other hidden fees that they do not fully understand or feel are fair. At the same time, they have been attracted by the personal relationships they build at locations like check cashers.[1] This is an opportunity for banking to reclaim that market and to provide consumers with better financial options.

Consider this: no one washes a rental car. Why take care of a car if there is no long-term benefit to the renter? The same applies to communities. We need to create a generation of individuals who see themselves as change agents and stakeholders, who care about the place where they live. This not only would help dispel blight and predatory practices in 500 credit score communities but also would help create stakeholders and a tax base.

Once again, we see that education really is the ultimate poverty eradication tool. When one knows better, one tends to do better.

CHAPTER SEVEN

The Power of Small Business and Entrepreneurship

Beginning in 2011, Gallup and Operation HOPE partnered on the first national poll of young people's behavioral economics, examining the interests of thirty million young people in fifth through twelfth grades. Among other things, the poll found that 77 percent of youth want to be their own boss, 45 percent want to own their own business, and 42 percent believe they will create something that changes the world. Ninety-one percent said they are not afraid to take risks and 91 percent said their minds never stopped. But only 5 percent of young people in the largest economy in the world are engaged in a business internship, and only about one-third of respondents had a parent or guardian who had ever started a business.[1]

In addition to economic literacy and access to credit and banking, America needs good jobs to foster a stable economic system, and we need to get on about the business of creating those. But these jobs are not going to come from traditional sources. Instead, we need a massive nationwide focus on entrepreneurship and small business creation, and a focus on the active development of what I call self-employment projects. Even when this focus does not in fact create entrepreneurs, it might succeed in creating something even more valuable in poor communities: an entrepreneurial, can-do, glass-is-half-full, let's-figure-out-what-we-are-for mind-set. Such a focus on empowerment rather than entitlement would be transformational in and of itself.

Take, for example, minority middle-class and upper-middle-class families. They are not complaining about racism and discrimination, but it is not because they are not experiencing any. The same is true of middle- and upper-middle-class Hispanic families or recently immigrated, now solid-middle-class and upper-middle-class Asian families, or the Jewish families that outran the rampant discrimination and torture of the Holocaust. Interestingly enough, this also applies to the previously rural white poor and working classes, who now see themselves transformed into the image of their "mainstream" middle- and upper-middle-class counterparts. These people are not complaining because they are too busy outrunning racism, discrimination, or both with replacement dreams of their own making.

A good job and the corresponding financial security and economic success it offers buys a whole lot of patience with garden-variety ignorance. With money in one's pocket, hope in one's heart, and opportunity filling one's head, it's easier to simply say "Whatever" and move on. Or, as my friend Van Jones recently said to me, with regard to the growing wave of minority youth violence in parts of Chicago and other low-wealth communities, "Nothing stops a bullet like a job."

An Untapped Well of Entrepreneurs

Like most law-abiding citizens, I hate criminal culture. The whole idea of the drug dealers and gangs I grew up around in Compton and South Central Los Angeles actually turns my stomach. I believe drug dealing is immoral and unethical and that there is a special place in hell reserved for anyone who sells death to his own people, in his own community, and in our schools.

Such people are helping to destroy the very community and family structure that I am trying to grow and sustain, but, unethical and immoral as their activities may be, I think criminals actually have the kind of skills that can help save poor communities in America, that they often represent a kind of untapped brilliance. After all, what is a so-called successful criminal if not an unethical American entrepreneur?

These people are not dumb. They understand import, export, wholesale, retail, markup, marketing, geography and territory, financing, and, of course, security. They understand how to take an idea and, with very few available resources, to make that idea real—maybe a bit too real—in people's lives. These are natural hustlers and entrepreneurs, but they have bad role models and a corrupt business model built on a form of "bad capitalism."

None of this is sustainable, none of it should happen, and, given that these people are not paying taxes on their ill-gotten gains, little of it will ever benefit our economy in the form of recorded gross domestic product or help our society by helping to fund the public good. But they often do succeed in creating a job for themselves and creating employment opportunities for others around them. To be a successful entrepreneur, one must be a contrarian; an out-of-the box thinker and doer; someone who takes risks; someone who is innovative, persistent, and hard-working; someone with a vision. These people have these traits.

Imagine if we could turn people with few opportunities but a lot of imagination into tomorrow's visionaries and entrepreneurs. This may represent a surprising way to harness the power of the American ideal, to foster small businesses and entrepreneurship, and to create jobs.

We're 650,000 Start-Ups Shy of a Revolutionary Tipping Point

According to Gallup research, 70 percent of all jobs in America come from small businesses with five hundred or fewer employees, and half of all jobs in America come from small businesses with one hundred or fewer employees. Jim Clifton adds, "There are approximately six million small businesses in the United States, and they are the very backbone of the country's democracy. Those businesses fund significantly more American jobs and [gross domestic product] than big business does."[2] For nearly eight years running, America hovered at around 400,000 start-ups per year, and most recently that number dipped troublingly to 350,000 in the last year reported. But, according to Clifton, we need approximately one million small business start-ups per year to lift up our country's economy, create jobs, and sustain our prosperity. That means we are about 650,000 start-ups short, and I believe that a good number of these small businesses can come from populations that have been left behind, ignored, or massively misunderstood and underestimated.

But the need for these small businesses is even more basic in the places and neighborhoods with which I am most concerned. These communities have enormous unmet needs for everything from traditional banking to gas stations to quality food and even entertainment. The U.S. Department of Agriculture's Economic Research Service estimated that 23.5 million people live in "food deserts" located more than one mile from a large grocery store.[3] More than half of these people (13.5 million) are low income, and thus there is a great need to set up markets and grocery stores in many communities. Meeting that need is one of the ways in which the poor can help save capitalism while also helping themselves.

And, of course, these communities also have untapped human capital—including those "unethical American entrepreneurs"—that can be leveraged in a number of directions to produce effective economic energy. So we are talking both an underserved consumer population for quality goods and services and an almost completely unrealized level of potential individual enterprise development.

Gallup–HOPE Index and Gallup Student Poll results for 2013 showed that today's low-income youth are more likely than their wealthier peers to develop problem-solving skills. In households earning less than $36,000 a year, about 47 percent of youth reported using their imagination every day at school, compared with 35 percent of youth from households earning $90,000 or more annually. Likewise, nearly 51 percent of youth from the lower-income household group reported learning new ways to solve problems at school, compared to

43 percent of youth from higher-earning households. The poll also showed that traditional minority groups have a higher propensity toward entrepreneurship than their mainstream counterparts.[4]

This makes perfect sense, because youth from low-wealth communities are forced to have much stronger coping skills to deal with difficult people and difficult situations, and, unfortunately, they are often forced to make adult decisions well before their time. Just as loss creates leaders, so too does this sort of sustained adversity management create and cultivate a personality that better manages less-than-perfect circumstances. These youth can turn the traditional challenges associated with low-wealth environments into a new strength, assuming that their spirits are not crushed in the process.

This of course means that these youth would make impressive employees for traditional employers, and there is a place for government to incentivize major corporations to establish appropriate business units, such as call centers, employing large numbers of people in these same communities.

But it also means that these youth would be great potential entrepreneurs. Given that youth and adults from low-wealth communities don't often have investable financial resources, their paid-in capital will typically come in the form of sweat equity and hustle. Jobs that rely heavily on these two attributes include sales and marketing (including multilevel marketing), a range of service businesses, and skilled professions such as plumbing and electrical services, construction, and carpentry.

Poor urban, inner-city, and rural communities have something else in common: you will find no Fortune 500 companies there. Mainstream and upscale communities have service providers on every corner, whereas the underserved communities I am talking about have unmet needs at every turn. The so-called experts argue that there is no money in these communities to purchase the items that such businesses are selling, but it is precisely the meeting of these needs that will unlock the buying power of these places—both current buying power, including money currently circulating in the underground economy, and the future buying power resulting from increased employment opportunities. Meeting these needs stabilizes communities, and this, along with good schools, attracts more residents. In this way, even the most low-tech businesses, the most basic enterprise development, and the smallest of enterprise operators can help to create jobs, increase gross domestic product, and stabilize communities.

Eric McLean's Plan for Success

Let's look at someone who has actually accomplished what I'm talking about. I recently met Eric McLean, a mobile notary public in Atlanta, who came by my office. As we signed documents I asked him how he became a notary. I assumed this was a part-time source of income for him. That's what I get for assuming.

McLean told me that he sort of stumbled into the business, beginning by paying the city $36 for a notary stamp. But he committed himself to working hard, and during his first month he made more than $1,000 in extra income. By his eighth month in business he was making $17,000 *per month!* By the time I spoke to him, McLean had ten mobile notaries working for him in and around Atlanta, another thirty-five mobile notaries in the state, and more than one hundred fifty mobile notaries in what he called his national network. He was writing more than one hundred fifty checks each month to small business owners across the nation who were making a full-time living as mobile notaries, all working through him.

But that wasn't all. McLean went on to tell me about his second business, insurance, and how he got into this business by recognizing that traditional auto insurance agents really don't like working past 5 or 6 P.M. on a workday evening, and almost never on the weekends. McLean recognized that most people likely purchase a car in the evenings or on weekends, so he opened a specialty practice that was open from 9 A.M. to 9 P.M. during the week, from noon to 9 P.M. on Saturdays, and a half day on Sundays. McLean cleaned up on all the business in this sector too.

McLean didn't try to cure cancer or create the newest Internet sensation. His business wasn't even what you would call sophisticated. He didn't spend a lot of start-up money, rent expensive office space, or lease a luxury car to impress clients or anyone else. His business cards don't identify him as the owner of his business; they simply say "mobile notary." Saying "CEO," he reasoned, didn't produce one additional happy client for his business.

McLean's plan for his simple business was in itself pretty simple. He found something that most everyone in his local area would need at some point, he invested $36 in himself and his dream, and then he got up the next morning—and every morning since—committed to doing the work. Real success does not have to be complicated when a commitment to work is present.

McLean also reminded me that his annual notary certification fee and all license fees for the year were effectively paid for by me in this single week. He thanked me and kept it moving.

A Generation of Leaders

What a man! A humble black man in casual slacks and a yellow polo shirt, wielding a $36 notary stamp and business cards without a title, generating $20,000 per month in business cash flow. We need a thousand more people like him, a generation of entrepreneurs, small business owners, and self-employment projects. This in turn will create a generation of jobs for urban, inner-city, and rural low-wealth neighborhoods. This is something everyone could do, in every community across the nation.

Doing this will also create taxpayers and stakeholders, which as we have noted is the key to funding infrastructure and good schools and to creating an environment in which the majority of a community's population is inclined to vote. It creates the entrepreneurial mind-set that can help poor communities to find hope, and this mind-set builds on itself, becoming more powerful with each generation. Both failure and success are cultures, and just as failure breeds more failure, success breeds more success.

So how do we motivate young people to embrace their entrepreneurial spirit and get to work on improving their lives and their communities? Although fear can work as a motivator to change human behavior, it's not all that effective, nor is it consistent. Aspiration, on the other hand, is much more effective in changing behavior. Aspiration is tied to hope itself.

There seems to be a disconnect between education and career today, with American youth getting more excited about being rich or being their own boss than about majoring in business or studying economics. Young people want one of two things to come as a result of their years committed to education: they either want to get a good job or they want to get a real shot at genuine economic opportunity, meaning they want to own or create or do something on their own. And in either pursuit they need the necessary skills, coupled with opportunity. We need to reconnect this aspiration with the education that enables young people to see the value of their schooling.

Kids are dropping out of high school in America for one principal reason—they don't believe that education is relevant to their future.[5] If we cannot convince young people that school can deliver either a job or a shot at economic opportunity, if they are not buying what schools are selling, forget about keeping them in school. We must reach these kids earlier and we must give them hope that, with their help, we can match their entrepreneurial aspirations with access to business internships and business role models. To do this, we must have a system to identify and educate these would-be entrepreneurs.

As Jim Clifton pointed out, the United States is extremely good at intellectual development. Our best schools and universities identify and nurture intellectual talent. If a student demonstrates a particularly high IQ, testing will identify that student, even in a poor or underserved neighborhood. And if a student is extremely gifted, he or she will probably be invited to attend the best universities and will even be given scholarships or financial aid. The same is true of people with exceptional athletic talent. But the system has no way of identifying someone with the skills that lend themselves toward entrepreneurship—for instance, determination, optimism, or problem-solving skills.

> Colleges and universities place tremendous weight on SAT or ACT scores. But nobody asks about the applicant's ability to start a company, build an organization, or create millions of customers. America leaves that to chance. . . . There are nearly 30 million students in U.S. middle and high schools right now. Early research in Gallup labs shows that about three in 1,000 working-age adults in the U.S. possess the rare talents of entrepreneurship. So that means there are potentially about 90,000 future "freaks of nature" out there. Let me take the liberty of rounding that number up to 100,000 potential blue chippers—potential entrepreneurs like Steve Jobs or Wayne Huizenga or Meg Whitman. America needs to find them all and make their entrepreneurial development as systematic and intentional as intellectual development is in this country.[6]

Even if the entrepreneurial path is not right for everyone, building these entrepreneurial skills in everyone—nurturing their hope, well-being, engagement, financial literacy, and economic energy—will supercharge their aspirations, their ambition, and their confidence levels. This in turn has the highest probability of creating a leadership generation.

The Path toward Long-Term Growth

To jump-start a stagnant U.S. economy and put the country on a path toward long-term economic growth and prosperity—

even global dominance once again—leaders must get their assumptions right. They must understand that entrepreneurship trumps innovation and that finding the next generation of great entrepreneurs means cultivating them in middle schools, high schools, colleges, and universities, just as surely and intentionally as the country cultivates innovators. Get these assumptions right and act on them, and America, rather than stagnating, declining, or flat-out going broke, will rise to new heights of global economic leadership. But entrepreneurship cannot be fostered by Washington; it must be developed at the city level.

We must find the one hundred thousand entrepreneurial "freaks of nature" and intentionally develop them like rare-IQ students and elite athletes. Next, we must identify high-potential small businesses and put them into power relationships with local mentors.

Creating those needed 650,000 new small businesses is precisely where the working poor, youth, and those in the middle class can help the most. Collectively, they have the will and the motivation to help America solve this problem, and, as the Gallup–HOPE Index noted, they have the natural aptitude and many of the natural skills. And there is even hope for the generation of young people who have been and unfortunately continue to get locked away as illegal entrepreneurs.

I urge banks to encourage community entrepreneurship in areas with depressed economies by granting loans that support small business and start-up growth in those areas. Perhaps then we will see more small businesses filling unmet needs in these areas and employing people in the community.

Role Models and Hope

In addition to developing people's talent and opening the way for entrepreneurship, we must encourage stronger community and business role modeling. People want to be respected and admired, but when their role models are nonexistent or negative, when their environment is horrible and contains few relationships to success and power, or when schools do not speak to their aspirations, a life of crime can seem alluring. And when the family unit is broken or nonexistent, the bonding and support inherent in a gang or criminal enterprise actually begins to look and feel like a family. All of this can be set straight, in part by offering people more positive role models.

All of us are who we are because of our role models. Whatever anyone has become in life, it began first with seeing that image somewhere. Being smart and working hard is not nearly enough if you don't have a relationship with a mentor or a model of life success.

I was a smart kid, sure of myself, and today I work hard, but I also am wise enough to know that I did not get to where I am all by myself. Like everyone, I had a lot of help along the way in the form of role models. I am a businessman today, for instance, because my father was a businessman who owned his own business for as long as I can remember. I love myself today because my mother told me she loved me every day as a child, and I absolutely believed it. Hope was made real in my life. In that sense, I was never poor. I just didn't have much money.

But my parents weren't the only role models in my com-

munity, and I saw my entire neighborhood essentially modeling two things: working for big businesses or government or,
unfortunately, the beginnings of what we may commonly refer
to today as thug culture. Either way, what I saw didn't seem to
add up to long-term success. I never saw the urban thugs grow
old and they never actually retired. They were either killed
or locked up for their activities. (In fact, they are still getting
locked up, and this has now become an industry all its own.)
Their stock-in-trade had no future; they were killing their customers. Clearly, this was not sustainable.

But the other route didn't seem to offer much, either. For
instance, my mother worked for McDonnell Douglas in Long
Beach, California, but I never knew anyone there who was
actually in charge of his or her own destiny. There were a lot
of bosses, whose titles said they were a manager, supervisor,
shift leader, union steward, and such. They had real authority
over other workers and they had some degree of control over
working conditions, all of which is important, but this was not
what I was looking for.

I kept looking for the people who had keys to the building,
not the department where my mother worked with her cowork-
ers. Who was the boss—the owner, entrepreneur, founder who
set up this entire enterprise? Who was the ultimate rule maker
and who earned the majority of the financial returns?

Likewise, while my friends were awestruck by star athletes
making millions of dollars a year, I wanted to know who had
enough wealth and power to actually pay fifteen star players
this kind of money, not to mention all the support staff and
costs. Respectfully, the players, amazing as they were, were all

employees. This other person was the *employer.* The players changed, but the owners, they just kept on rolling.

I wanted to know how this system worked. I wanted to know who had the power to do all of this, and how they got it. I wanted to unpack this economic power and repack it with the poor people I knew in mind.

Aspiration and Opportunity

A study by the University of Chicago, cited in Malcolm Gladwell's *The Tipping Point,* noted that it only takes 5 percent of a community to act as role models to stabilize a community.[7] I find it amazing that only 5 percent of a community needs to stand up and show young people in their lives the path to a successful career in order to trigger an economic tipping point that can stabilize a neighborhood and eventually a nation!

This is why Operation HOPE forged a partnership with Gallup to institute a one hundred–year study to measure entrepreneurial potential and opportunity in youth. After two years of data, the Gallup–HOPE Index has shown that, although 77 percent of students want to be their own boss, only 5 percent are currently learning the skills necessary to do so by interning with a local business.[8] What would happen if we could connect 5 percent of adults in low-wealth communities to the 5 percent learning the skills necessary to become entrepreneurs? Better yet, what if we could prepare 20 percent of students to be entrepreneurs and then connected that even larger population with adult mentors?

If the so-called poor could access a broader base of role

models, business internships right out of high school or even middle school, and a corresponding new image of themselves, others would begin to view them through a new lens as well. Their new image would be one of opportunity and aspiration rather than of poverty and despair. And imagine if they had new tools to go along with this new perspective; a different culture of entrepreneurship, small business ownership, and job creation; a culture of creating something for themselves, by themselves.

Present estimates indicate that 20 percent to 50 percent of students in many large urban high schools fail to graduate, in part because many students don't believe their education is connecting them to a sustainable career. Students who do not complete high school have lower overall expected life outcomes, including lower lifetime earnings, lower rates of employment, decreased health, and higher incarceration rates.[9] Thus, dropping out and being underattached to the economy has a negative effect not just on that former student but also on society as a whole, and it carries a large taxpayer burden. The California Dropout Research Project has found that high school dropouts from the class of 2007 alone will cost the state $46.4 billion over the course of their lifetimes.[10] These costs included lost earnings, lower economic growth, lower tax revenues, and higher government spending.[11]

We must connect this next generation with a meaningful role in the workforce, through more private sector mentorship, cradle-to-career pathways, and positive role modeling in schools and communities. We can get students excited about the connection between their education, their ambitions, and their potential career, and each of us can be a role model in our own community and in the lives of those around us. The job of our generation will be to connect the 45 percent of youth who want to start their own businesses with more mentors and internships, so that more than 5 percent of them can have the job training and mentorship necessary to embark on a successful career.

If we can connect aspiration with career opportunity through increased role modeling for youth, everything could be different. Instead of finding failing schools in economic dead zones, inner-city and low-wealth communities would be red-hot emerging markets providing value-added growth in America. This is our task, and this is our moment.

PART IV

HARVESTING HOPE

CHAPTER EIGHT

The HOPE Plan

Following World War II, the United States put together an initiative to provide economic and technical support to help Europe rebuild its cities and economies. Called the European Recovery Program but popularly known as the Marshall Plan, after Secretary of State George Marshall, the plan was designed to modernize European industry and remove trade barriers, in addition to revitalizing destroyed cities and putting people back to work.

The program began in April 1948, ran for four years, and was an unqualified success. Those four years of American technical and financial assistance may not have been solely responsible for Europe's recovery, but it certainly helped, and most leaders today would probably agree that this not only was the right thing to do at the time but also was smart politics and even smarter economics. We are still benefiting from the effects of the Marshall Plan, and our former enemy Germany is today one of the world's largest, most vital economies as well as one of our principal allies and largest trading partners. (The same is true of Japan, to whom the United States also offered assistance.)

Perhaps most important, America gained global moral

authority by undertaking this plan, and for the first time it became a global leader. After the bombs came an activist agenda of dignity, prosperity, and opportunity for all, both here and abroad. This wasn't a Democrat answer or a Republican answer. It was a successful American answer. The global economic system that we all now enjoy rides on the back of that acquired soft power.

Today, bringing hope to the U.S. economy calls for an economic Marshall Plan for our times. Call it the HOPE Plan. Its armies are the least of these, and the command staff are American and global business leaders, backed by government leaders with both vision and courage. The mission is nothing less than lifting up the working poor, the underserved, and the struggling middle class and offering them the tools, the road map, and the inspiration to reclaim their lives and a society that actually works for all. The original Marshall Plan rebuilt shattered cities; this plan must rebuild hopes, dreams, and a commonsense pathway toward a shared future prosperity, before we build one new road, bridge, or building. In fact, if we don't do the former, the latter won't mean much.

The HOPE Plan for rebuilding America includes things that can be done right now—by our government, yes, but more specifically by each of us. These potentially game-changing actions to steer us toward a more prosperous and inclusive union are practical and are within our reach, enabling all of us to contribute to the fulfillment of the promise of the U.S. Constitution and our Bill of Rights, that every American will enjoy life, liberty, and the pursuit of happiness. Not some of us. All of us.

Financial Literacy and Financial Access

As we've seen, making a place at the table for the poor and underserved begins with financial literacy and everything that goes with it, including access to banking, improved credit scores, and ownership of homes or other real estate. These measures work toward those goals.

▸ **Advocate federally funded financial literacy education for every child in the nation, from kindergarten through college.** We cannot expect people to participate in a financial system that is a mystery to them, and an inability to function in our increasingly finance-oriented world is a serious hindrance for people who have not been given the basic tools of financial literacy. The common core curriculum currently adopted by forty-six states and the District of Columbia is a terrific vehicle for delivering financial literacy alongside subjects such as basic mathematics. Amy Rosen, Beth Kobliner, and the President's Advisory Council on Financial Capability have devised a blueprint for this work, called the Money as You Grow model.[1]

▸ **Establish access to banking as a legal human right for every American, at birth.** Keeping an estimated forty million underbanked and ten million unbanked American households[2] outside of the mainstream banking system is more punitive to them and to our national economic health than simply allowing them low-risk access to universal debit card–based banking. In addition to exposing millions of people in low-wealth communities to unscrupulous providers of nontraditional financial services, the lack of a bank account carries a host of other consequences. For instance, many Hurricane Katrina victims could not receive Federal Emergency Management Agency payments because they did not have a bank account to accept funds, and participation in the new Affordable Care Act will require either a bank account or some other acceptable form of mainstream financial access. Ensuring a bank account for all will directly link financial literacy with financial capability for every American citizen.

▸ **Improve credit scores in 500 credit score communities.** As we've seen, a poor credit score affects every aspect of a person's life and, by extension, their community. Inability to access credit creates easy marks for unscrupulous lending, makes it impossible to own a home, and may even affect one's ability to get a job. Raising the credit scores of people in 500 credit score communities not only benefits individuals but also has the power to transform entire communities.

▸ **Create middle-class tax breaks and low wealth–family incentives to purchase homes and invest in and rehabilitate dormant local real estate.** Home ownership provides low-income and middle-class families with financial stability and a stake in a community. We should foster people's ability to participate in home ownership through Dignity Mortgages or similar programs.

▸ **Direct the U.S. Department of the Treasury and the Internal Revenue Service to auto-debit the Earned Income Tax**

Credit for all individuals and families who qualify. Many low-income people don't even realize they qualify for this federally funded credit for working people.

▸ **Build financial wellness and financial literacy into corporate culture and employer human resource departments.** Investing in the workforce by providing people with financial literacy will pay measurable returns to employers, including improved employee well-being and engagement, which will help employees feel that they are thriving. These and other employer actions on behalf of employees will help to reduce employee stress levels, which often increases morale.[3]

Employment and Entrepreneurship

In addition to establishing financial literacy and empowerment, we need to create opportunities and incentives for employment and entrepreneurship. HOPE Plan elements here include job creation and entrepreneurship initiatives.

▸ **Create private sector tax breaks and incentives to provide business internships directly after high school graduation.** If we could provide a paid internship for every youth who achieves a passing grade in high school, we might be able to crush the high school dropout epidemic in America. All young people really want as a result of education is a good job or a shot at economic opportunity. Providing such an opportunity in the form of internships would help solve several problems, including a reduction of the average $37,440 that each youth dropout costs the nation each year.[4]

▸ **Establish public equity funding and/or public–private matching incentives for the creation of small business and entrepreneurial start-ups.** This could build on the Small Business Administration's Small Business Investment Company program and the JOBS Act crowd funding legislation passed in 2012.

▸ **Fire American innovation at every level of society.** Place a U.S. patent office in every low-wealth community. Incentivize a culture in low-wealth communities to radically increase the ideas-to-patent culture and experience.

▸ **Institute a national infrastructure revitalization plan to repair, revitalize, and rebuild our nation's roads, bridges, rail systems, and ports.** Our national infrastructure is in great need of repair and our people need jobs. Matching up this need with the opportunity to employ people is good for individuals, good for our country, and good for the economy.

Nurturing Human Capital

Ensuring that the first two parts of the HOPE Plan succeed requires that certain baseline human capital needs are met. Fostering education, boosting kids' self-esteem, providing role models, and creating environmental sustainability are the enabling conditions for everything else in the plan.

▸ **Make an absolute commitment to a right-sized and sub-sidized education for all.** Having an educated population is not a privilege or a luxury; it is a necessity for future and sustained national economic growth and the stability of our democracy. And it's less expensive than more law enforcement. Today, however, our education system is failing us. Poor communities have poor schools with not enough teachers, scant enrichment programs, and supply shortages. And even when primary and high school education is adequate, the oppressive stranglehold of student loans and its accompanying debt has become an effective brake on the aspirations and overall development of young people and new families. We must commit to providing all of our citizens with free, quality educational opportunities.

» **Adopt an inclusive growth strategy.** If a company or government entity wants to be effective, viable, and sustainable as it grows, it must incorporate all members of its community. America is successful in part because it strives to be inclusive of all peoples and races, and in general it benefits from this policy and approach. California and New York, for instance, are the largest economies in the United States, and they also happen to be the most ethnically diverse states. Encouraging every company and local government to adopt its own version of an inclusive growth (diversity) strategy would bring more of those outside the mainstream economy into it and would help to drive continued growth. Diversity is not only a moral issue but also simply smart business.

» **Focus on transformation rather than simple incarceration of the nonviolent prison population.** Instead of locking people up for nonviolent offenses and creating people who often find it nearly impossible to find a job after being released with a criminal record, we should encourage and incentivize job programs of all sorts, including entrepreneurship, small business, and self-employment project initiatives. Education makes a whole lot more sense for the country's long-term prospects.

▸ **Create an incentive and tax breaks for all Americans to volunteer as a role model in their communities at least once a month.** Businesses should reward employees for volunteering (as many do) and for mentorship and role modeling in their communities.

▸ **Establish environmental sustainability as a new cultural norm.** Create tax breaks and incentives for employers, families, and individuals who embark upon a holistic path of environmental sustainability in the form of energy savings and/or green job creation.

▸ **Create a public chief opportunity officer post within every federal, state, and local government agency.** The poor do not have a lobbyist, so the mission of opportunity officers would be the promotion of opportunity for all by looking at the activities of various government agencies and how they might be amplified, modified, restructured, or realigned to provide jobs and economic opportunities. Ideally, opportunity officers would be former and retired CEOs from the private sector, and others with experience in job and opportunity creation.

What America and, by extension, the world has been dealing with since 2006 is not really just an economic crisis. The crisis is merely showing itself economically because we now live in a largely economic world. Instead, this is really a crisis of virtues and values. We have hit a wall. This is not America in recession; it is America on reset. We have in front of us, right now, a once-in-a-century opportunity to change everything.

This HOPE Plan is a big idea that seeks not merely to include the poor, to be moral and kind, or to placate the ever-growing struggling middle class. It is a bold plan to fuse the huddled masses with the future success of this nation. It is the remaking of America that actually saves America.

Operation HOPE is specifically focused on what Dr. King referred to as the third phase of the civil rights movement, or the Poor People's Campaign, which he chronicled in his final book, *Where Do We Go from Here: Chaos or Community?*, and launched in earnest in 1968.[5] Dr. King was killed in Memphis, Tennessee, during the first march of this movement, but we are still asking ourselves some of these same questions nearly fifty years later.

With the launch of this next phase of work, which operates at a national scale but aims at measurable local impact, we seek to answer some of these questions. The HOPE Plan is intended to inject into society a real, tangible, and practical plan of action in which most everyone can play a meaningful role.

CHAPTER NINE

Project 5117

Project 5117 is Operation HOPE's revolutionary four-pronged approach to combating economic inequality. Project 5117 programs improve financial literacy, increase the ratio of business role models and business internships from today's national average of 5 percent to 20 percent, and stabilize the American dream by empowering adults and families to become involved in the banking system and to help to raise their credit scores.[1] This project is being rolled out throughout America in 2014 and by 2020 will reach the following benchmarks:

- We must begin by empowering **five million youth** with a new level of financial literacy through unique financial dignity education programs that already have been successfully taught in 3,500 schools across the country. The program ensures basic consumer protection education for a generation, while making smart cool so kids stay in school.

- Next, we must help **one million** of these students become future entrepreneurs and local job creators through HOPE Business in a Box academies, sponsored by a one hundred–year partnership with Gallup Inc. This effort powerfully reconnects education with aspiration in the lives of our youth. Two thousand HOPE Business in a Box academies are planned across the nation, in both urban and rural communities.

▸ Third, in order to provide families with access to banking, we are establishing **one thousand bottom-up branch banks** (empowerment centers) throughout America, through a program called HOPE Inside, as well as five thousand certified locations, through HOPE Inside Plus. This plan is entirely consistent with the long-term growth strategies of major banks and builds on the existing branch banking network across America.

▸ Finally, to achieve the goal of **increasing credit scores to a bankable level of 700**, we will target those earning $50,000 or less annually. This group comprises the working poor, the working class, and the struggling middle class.

Project 5117 is about changing and transforming an entire generation, empowering future leaders for America, and stabilizing and rooting this generation of working poor, working-class, and middle-class communities, first by addressing the untapped power of business role models and business internships for youth and then by creating opportunities for those families to participate in banking and credit.

Five Million Kids

Let's start with five million fourth- through twelfth-graders nationwide. Five Million Kids, or 5MK for short, is cochaired by entertainment icon Quincy Jones and civil rights icon Andrew Young, with support from other key 5MK ambassadors, such as "hip-hop chairman" Russell Simmons, actor and comedian Chris Tucker, and a growing list of other leaders in entertainment and sports.

If you want to put a kid from a low-wealth community to sleep, give him or her a traditional financial literacy course. This is why we are branding 5MK around the likeness and image of participating celebrities, to help make the whole thing cool. We started with Jones, introducing his Banking on Our Future, Quincy Jones Celebrity Edition curriculum into Quincy Jones Elementary School in South Los Angeles. Soon we will include the schools and neighborhoods where Jones grew up, around Chicago and Seattle. These are areas of passionate concern and interest to Jones, and the Operation HOPE team will do the year-round school work because that's what we are passionate about.

5MK brings together our Course in Dignity, which encourages values and self-esteem building, with the basics of checking, savings, credit, investment, and the history of banking and finance. This is all wrapped around and made personal to the kids through the life stories of larger-than-life celebrities they admire and respect.

This Banking on Our Future celebrity support will power the 5MK work on the ground and in local schools. We will recruit celebrity leaders from a broad cross section of culture, geography, race, and gender and will replicate Banking on Our Future in other underserved communities across America. The celebrity leadership community gets to leverage its greatest talents and skills, and Operation HOPE gets to leverage ours.

One Million Youth

Out of the population of five million kids targeted for the first phase of our culture-transformation work, we will focus on one million, from 2013 to 2020, to play a leadership role in our HOPE Business in a Box academies. Our plan is to set up two thousand of these academies in the approximately one hundred thousand public schools in urban and rural communities around America. This 2 percent market penetration is all we need to spark this movement, which will give us cultural concentration in the communities most in need.

A HOPE Business in a Box academy is like taking a private school's resource library and placing it in a public school. It starts with the young people who have already gone through our baseline Banking on Our Future program and then builds on this by running them through a primer course in entrepreneurship, whether this is Operation HOPE's curriculum, the National Foundation for Teaching Entrepreneurship's curriculum, or the curriculum of the U.S. Small Business Administration's Office of Entrepreneurship Education.

Operation HOPE has innovated twenty-five small businesses that a young person can create on his or her own for under $500. Innovation can sprout in the form of a local neighborhood lemonade stand, a candy shop (my first business), or a mobile application in the App Store or Android Market. Program participants come up with their own business ideas and then prepare to go on stage to make a two-minute pitch before a local group of business leaders, who also act as role models. Think *Shark Tank* for children.

The winners of the pitch competition are awarded $500

grants, and the rest of the HOPE Business in a Box participants are encouraged to leverage their existing social networks
to gain money for their business using the HOPE Business in
a Box crowdsourcing platform, which enables youth to engage
their friends and family in supporting their business. The
platform also enables youth to request contacts, access to the
networks of successful individuals in their desired field, or
nonmonetary resources for the launch of their business.

Imagine how these young people's brains are just firing off
with optimism, hope, opportunity, and a sense of aspiration
for themselves. Maybe for the first time, someone is looking at
them, investing time in them, taking them seriously.

Consider a school with a population of one thousand kids
who all went through the baseline financial literacy course
work. Let's say maybe six hundred to eight hundred of those
same kids completed the entrepreneurship course work, and
maybe two hundred to three hundred completed the course
work on starting a business for $500 or less. Finally, of those
two hundred to three hundred young people, maybe only fifty
to one hundred kids actually pitch twice a year in their school
auditorium.

This nonetheless spells success, because all we need is 5
percent of these young people—fifty or more out of one thousand—to ultimately engage in the most visible and most powerful initiative in that school to change lives. That 5 percent
can serve as role models, stabilizing the school. The young
people, teachers, families, and local business professionals
and owners who attend these pitch events all are playing
as powerful a role as the kids on stage pitching their ideas.
This program will build on its own momentum, setting off

a chain reaction of entrepreneurship, mentorship, and business opportunity.

This is not really about trying to create entrepreneurs, though many will be created in and through this process. Nor is it about achieving a return on investment—that's why Operation HOPE gives business grants and not business loans. Instead, we are trying to change the prevailing culture in a school, to make it cool and viable to follow your dreams and initiative. We firmly believe this will create a new generation of leaders for America's future.

Just imagine what might be possible if we could turn potential dropouts and chronically unemployed people into engines for growth and wealth. If we are even remotely successful in churning out anywhere close to one million young HOPE Business in a Box entrepreneurs and small business owners, the chain reaction and change in culture would be larger than Operation HOPE; such a change would affect America.

One Thousand Branch Banks

In addition to creating kids with the vision to become entrepreneurs, we must enable those same kids and their families to access banking and improve their credit scores. Operation HOPE's vision for creating access to banking is called HOPE Inside—HOPE Inside bank branches, HOPE Inside credit unions, HOPE Inside grocery stores and big box retailers. Our strategy envisions the deployment of more than one thousand bottom-up branch banks, called empowerment centers, throughout America. HOPE Inside aims to access a very reasonable and attainable 1 percent of the mainstream banking branch network.

Apart from this, we also are launching HOPE Inside Plus, which involves licensing branches as well as training and certifying bank branch employees to become authorized HOPE financial literacy counselors. The network would be both a "private banker" for the working poor, the underserved, and the struggling middle class and a national banking and empowerment network to serve those with annual incomes of $50,000 or less.

We have launched the HOPE Inside network with a national partnership with SunTrust Banks, one of the top ten U.S. banks, whose chairman and CEO Bill Rogers is leading the company's inspired purpose: "Lighting the way to financial well-being." A number of other top corporate brand leaders also have signed on, including Accenture, Bank of the West (an early innovator), City National Bank, the City of Miami, Equifax, the Federal Deposit Insurance Corporation, Microsoft, OneWest Bank, Popular Community Bank, Regions Financial Corporation, the Small Business Administration, and Union Bank, among others.

Our goal for HOPE Inside Plus is to enlist five thousand trained and certified bankers, which translates into another 2,500 or more service locations, for a total of 3,500 service and empowerment locations for low-wealth, working-poor, working-class, and struggling middle-class individuals, families, communities, and small businesses. Another two thousand school-based locations will empower at-risk youth with their own economic energy, tying education back to youth aspiration.

Credit Scores of 700

Other than perhaps love and God, nothing changes a person's life more than raising his or her credit score by 120 points. To that end, Operation HOPE is launching a 700 credit score initiative in communities where the average credit score is 500 to 550, which formerly has doomed them to the indignity of predatory subprime lenders, check cashers, title lenders, pay-day loans, and rent-to-own-stores. We have launched HOPE 700 Credit Score Communities at all of our HOPE Center locations across the nation, and we will focus on moving credit scores not just for our clients but also in and for the communities that surround our centers.

We have found that we can and consistently do help our clients raise their credit scores by more than one hundred points, and when a counseling client moves his or her credit score to 670 or more, everything in that person's life changes. Her financial literacy changes, her sense of well-being and hope goes through the roof, and her engagement in her own life rises to a new level, matching her new financial skill set.

In an effort to root our work in moral authority, we are beginning in and around the HOPE Financial Dignity Center at Ebenezer Baptist Church in Atlanta, Georgia, the moral home of Dr. King. Operation HOPE is presently the anchor tenant for the Martin Luther King Sr. Community Resource Complex at Ebenezer and on the larger King Center campus in Atlanta, Georgia. The HOPE center at Ebenezer will be the centralized national location for training, certification, inspiration, and innovation. This is all part of the new Operation

HOPE "software of human development" to lift credit scores, and with it, human potential.

America 2020

America 2020 is the local rollout of Project 5117. There will be a Denver 2020, a New York 2020, a Los Angeles 2020, and so on until we have reached all underserved communities and brought them the benefits of Project 5117. America 2020 is our national campaign to change lives home by home, street by street, school by school, and community by community. When we launch this campaign to save our children, we also excite and inspire the American experience of democracy and freedom itself. When we advance this cause, we are speaking to the highest ideas and ideals referenced by Dr. King and others who proclaimed their movement to be about redeeming the soul of America.

This national campaign, beginning in local communities, is of the people, by the people, and for the people. It is not about race or the color line but about class and poverty. As so many movements for change are, this movement will be led by young people helping the country find its way, but it also will be led by Americans helping youth to find their way to a meaningful, dignified role in the economy. It will be accomplished in the streets but also the suites, from public school classrooms to school board hearing rooms. This campaign will connect the power and history of the civil rights movement with the promise and future opportunity of a silver rights movement.

Ideas, Tools, and People

Other notable and credible leaders have worked to ensure that the poor and severely underserved have basic access to the seed capital they need to run a business in villages throughout the developing world, through the bottom-up approach of microcredit and microfinance. At Operation HOPE, we have a different vision. We have sought to positively attack and to break down the remaining barriers to the remaining global sector that has never truly been commoditized and opened up to all: banking and financial services. This critical industry is a fundamental driver of gross domestic product growth globally, and we seek to commoditize its access, opportunity, and availability here and around the world.

We have no interest in creating what would effectively be a parallel universe of financial services for the poor, which is what microcredit and microfinance could possibly become if the industry's politics and growth strategies are not handled and managed just right going forward. Instead, we seek to mainstream banking and financial services for the poor, the underserved, and even the struggling middle class, to work with mainstream banking and financial services and government to return banking to the people.

However, Operation HOPE will not be able to do this alone. In fact, in order for this plan to succeed it will have to include the broadest coalition of collaborative partners, representing the private sector, government, and communities, and with ongoing engagement from and with the media. Operation HOPE will be reaching out continually and on an ongoing basis to leaders across the spectrum to substantively engage them in this work.

It is critically important that neither Operation HOPE nor anyone else is viewed as "owning" this movement and work. Operation HOPE can provide some of the initial ideas and tools, but others engaged with the movement will also add their own unique twist to the work. Most important, it will be the people, from all walks of life, who will bring the magic to the movement. An effort this large will not be defined by any single announcement, press conference, partner, or undertaking. But all of its relevant parts, partners, people, and ongoing progress will give it substance and sustainable energy over time.

For instance, in an effort to tell the story of this work, its impact, and its outcomes, the leading brand management firm BBDO in New York has agreed to take the lead on a brand awareness campaign tied to the HOPE Business in a Box crowdsourcing backend mechanism of youth business funding. Likewise, the leading public relations firm Qorvis has agreed to take the lead in telling the site-by-site human interest success stories that are part and parcel of the national HOPE Inside objective of moving individuals toward 700 credit scores.

In an effort to resource support for the work, Operation HOPE has launched a formal road show for both America 2020 and the HOPE Inside models, which will continue through December 2020. This effort is beginning nationally and will quickly move to the level of city-by-city leadership engagement. To supply boots-on-the-ground troop strength, Operation HOPE will rely on its growing HOPE Corps, presently 22,000 strong, with an eventual goal of one hundred thousand trained, certified professionals to act as volunteers and business role models. At present, the HOPE Fellows, Interns, Loaned Executives, and Volunteer Executives program includes one hundred members and is growing; our eventual goal is to have five hundred members actively engaged with this work.

Dr. King's dream was focused on redeeming the soul of America, not (just) fighting injustice. In that way, his work was aspirational, and so will this work be. America 2020 and Project 5117 will help to build stronger communities that contribute to a growing, economically stable America. In the final analysis, the real and sustainable vision driving this new silver rights movement is the work.

Where We Go from Here

People seem genuinely confused about how the poor get out of this mess. I am not. In many ways, I am building upon the solid foundations of thoughtful global leadership focused on poverty eradication advanced by such people as Dr. Muhammad Yunus, founder of Grameen Bank, and C. K. Prahalad, author of *The Fortune at the Bottom of the Pyramid*.[1] And although I believe my approach is applicable in many places around the world, I am mainly focused on the unique brand of American poverty as it exists today, and my tone and approach are possibly more radical than theirs, because the poverty question in America is more challenging to define.

America's poverty is not just about money and not having enough of it. In America, issues of money and good decision making are often wrapped up and mixed up with issues of individual self-esteem and confidence, community culture and belief systems, values, and, quite frankly, emotional and psychological depression. But the core of the problem is the same: Poor people have more time than money in their days and not enough tangible opportunity in their lives. They pay the most to get the poorest quality goods and services, and all too often they feel beaten down before they even get started with their day. Bad capitalism then feeds on this sense of despair, cynicism, and lack of hope.

In addition, you don't find a lot of big businesses operating in urban, inner-city, or poor and struggling rural communities, and big businesses often don't create many new jobs. And because of the heavy reliance on government programs, the perception of government as savior is heavier than it should be in these same communities, given that only about 9 percent of all American jobs come from the government.[2] The government plays a significant subsidy role in the lives of the poor, but it doesn't often play a sustainable employment role.

The Next Big Bang of Global Economic Growth

So, while the world is still adjusting to and trying to recover from the worst global economic crisis since the Great Depression, I am focused on what comes next. In the midst of this crisis I also see an opportunity to finally make free enterprise and responsible capitalism relevant to and workable for the poor and the underserved. This time around, world economic growth will require the positive inclusion of us all.

The United States has seen four major "big bangs" in economic growth in its history: an agricultural phase, an industrial phase, a technology phase, and our present information age. These previous stages of economic growth required land, buildings, equipment, or other "things" to light the fuse of economic growth and prosperity. Even the information age, which we currently are in and have arguably led, has depended upon the thing called a microprocessor.

Our next economic big bang, the fifth stage of economic

prosperity, will be very different. Rather than relying on things, it will rely almost wholly on what we might call the "software of human development." This is the development and unleashing of empowered human capital around the world. The new software of human development is what arises when you energize and inspire a generation of young people with the power of a new, transformational idea. The idea is this: you are the product. And when people know this, when they believe this, when they are given the tools and opportunity to achieve this, they become what I call "the CEO of you."

Three Brothers Just Working

Following my recent wedding, part of which took place at our home, my personal assistant's three teenage sons came over to help out with some of the cleanup and reorganizing. All three young men were hard working, focused, intelligent, and did excellent work. They also lacked permanent, full-time jobs. They did excellent work for me, so I could not understand why they were not gainfully employed.

In talking to them, I learned about a number of factors that might have affected their employment chances. For instance, they had opted out of going to college, which might have helped, although pursuing a college education assumes that one can actually find a job after graduation, which is not guaranteed. They also did not have many connections with successful people who might like, trust, and want to help them. They just really had no foothold to begin their journey upward.

So I suggested that these three young men turn their problem or challenge into an opportunity, just as Ryan Taylor had in founding DROBE and Eric McLean had in setting up his notary business. When and if you cannot find a job, go create one. I suggested that they create a new business called Three Brothers Just Working, with a Web site telling their stories, giving background on each of them and their families, and explaining how supporting this business enterprise not only was enabling them to provide real value to customers and their community but also was lifting the boats of three very specific young men.

With my new wife and I serving as references, I suggested they consider starting right on my block, walking door to door with their soon-to-be-created small business services brochure, respectfully offering to do a first job of up to three hours for free for each new client (knowing that almost no person in my neighborhood would ever allow these bright and hard-working young men to work for free). I told them that after their first five or ten clients, the next ten would roll in through references, in short order.

"Wouldn't it be cool," I said, "if within a few years you're employing some of your neighborhood friends?"

They agreed that this would be very cool. They looked excited, though a little scared.

Finally, I told them that Operation HOPE and our HOPE Financial Dignity Center would be happy to provide them with free entrepreneurship and small business training classes, to help them with their business plan. Now the look of doubt and fright was replaced with a little confidence. They wouldn't be in this alone.

And with that short conversation, hope was restored in the lives of three young black men who were on the bubble of life in America. With just a little push in a positive direction, they saw that they could become entrepreneurs, small business owners, taking care of their responsibilities, generating economic energy, creating jobs (starting with jobs for themselves), and helping to save America.

This is the master plan for every low-wealth community in America, and arguably throughout the world, that lacks sufficient real-time economic energy: go create some of your own. After all, every big business was once a small one.

What the world needs now is a generation endowed with the empowered human capital to create its own jobs. And when they do this—when one billion youth around the world figure out how they can light the creative fuse to lift themselves up through self-determination—they not only help secure the gross domestic product growth that the world needs but also gain dignity for themselves and all those around them. This is how the poor can save capitalism.

Detroit's Young Derrick Is My Hope

Derrick lives in Detroit's inner city and was about ten years old when I heard about him through our HOPE Global Youth Empowerment Group division. Derrick's school was participating in our six-session Banking on Our Future financial literacy course, led by volunteer professionals. The volunteer who visited Derrick's class obviously did a good job of unpacking capitalism and explaining the global language of money, and Derrick, in particular, was captivated.

By the third class session, young Derrick was punching a hole in the air with his hand, asking pointed questions of the volunteer banker. By the fifth session, he was wearing to class the only suit he owned, emulating the look of this successful role model. Derrick's classmates, of course, teased him for this at first. Nonetheless, by the time he graduated from the six-week class, Derrick was on fire with a new vision for himself.

As Derrick was walking down the school hallway after the final class, two of his "friends" approached, once again teasing him about the suit and now asking why he was hanging around with "those people." The banker happened to overhear. He approached the group and, to make a point, offered to give each of the three $70 and three minutes to make a decision about the company Nike.

Derrick's two friends immediately decided they would each buy a pair of Nike's Air Jordan basketball shoes, although they would each need an additional $30 to do so. Young Derrick, on the other hand, immediately decided that he would buy one share of Nike stock, which was trading at around $64 at the time, yielding him $6 in change!

Now, it was amazing enough that Derrick already knew that he could buy one share of Nike stock for less than $70. Even many adults don't know this kind of thing. But the real amazing part was yet to come.

Derrick's friends starting razzing him, saying, "Man, why do you want to buy some stupid stock? You want to get some cool Air Jordans. Everyone in school has Air Jordans," and so on. Peer pressure at work. In fact, they were getting on Derrick so bad and so loudly that the adult volunteer asked him if he was going to be OK.

Derrick's response was immediate: "I'm good, man. And I

want them to buy those shoes. Because when they do, they're making me money."

Boom. That's it. There's that burning branch. That moment when that light of hope comes on, and it's not turning off anytime soon.

There may come a time, soon, when young Derrick will be without money in his pocket. Maybe his family will be broke, too. But Derrick will never, ever be poor again. He has banished that failed poverty mentality from his life forever.

And this is my hope: to create a generation of young Derricks, all across America, one household, one classroom, one school, one street, one neighborhood, and one city at a time. Remember, we only need 5 percent of a community to serve as role models to stabilize that community.

I want an entire community of young leaders like Derrick. Young people who don't think like me but think for themselves. Young people who, maybe for the first time in their lives, are hopeful and focused on their education, their aspiration, their opportunity, their dream for a better life and a better world.

It can be done.

NOTES

Chapter 1: Separate, Unequal America

1. Data from World Bank, "GDP (current US$)," http://data. worldbank.org/indicator/NY.GDP.MKTP.CD.

2. Josh Boak, "U.S. Unemployment Aid Surges to 368,000," *ABC News*, December 12, 2013.

3. Karen E. Dynan, Jonathan Skinner, and Stephen P. Zeldez, "Do the Rich Save More?," *Journal of Political Economy* 112, no. 2 (2004).

4. E. N. Wolff, "Changes in Household Wealth in the 1980s and 1990s in the U.S." (working paper no. 407, Annandale-on-Hudson, NY: The Levy Economics Institute of Bard College, 2004).

5. Federal Deposit Insurance Corporation, *2011 FDIC National Survey of Unbanked and Underbanked Households* (Washington, DC: Federal Deposit Insurance Corporation, September 2012).

6. Ed Garsten, "GM Healthcare Bill Tops $60 Billion," *Detroit News*, March 11, 2004.

7. Nancy Harty, "5 Dead, 26 Wounded, in Weekend Shootings," *Chicago Sun–Times*, June 18, 2012.

8. Statistics from mint.com cited in Chris Preston, "Five Reasons Professional Athletes Go Broke," *Wyatt Investment Research*, March 5, 2013.

9. Shane J. Lopez, "Making Hope Happen in the Classroom," *Phi Delta Kappan* 95, no. 2 (October 2013): 19–22. See also Allie Grasgreen, "Here's Hoping," *Inside Higher Ed*, July 6, 2012.

Chapter 2: A New Look at Income Disparity

1. United States Census Bureau, "Poverty," http://www.census.gov/ hhes/www/poverty/data/threshld/index.html.

2. Jacob S. Hacker, *The Great Risk Shift: The New Insecurity and the Decline of the American Dream* (New York: Oxford University Press, 2006).

3. See Lawrence Mishel, "Markets, Wages, and Fighting Poverty," *The Economic Policy Institute Blog*, January 8, 2014, http://www.epi.org/blog/markets-wages-fighting-poverty; and Paul Wiseman, "Richest 1 Percent Earn Biggest Share since '20s," *Associated Press*, September 10, 2013.

4. Angela Johnson, "76% of Americans Are Living Paycheck-to-Paycheck," *CNN Money*, June 24, 2013.

5. Mitra Toossi, "Consumer Spending: An Engine of US Job Growth," *Monthly Bureau of Labor Review*, November 2002, http://www.bls.gov/opub/mlr/2002/11/art2full.pdf.

6. Anandi Mani, "Poverty Impedes Cognitive Function," *Science* 341, no. 6149 (2013): 976–980.

7. Society for Human Resource Management, *Background Checking— The Use of Credit Background Checks in Hiring Decisions*, July 19, 2012, http://www.shrm.org/Research/SurveyFindings/Articles/Pages/Credit BackgroundChecks.aspx.

8. Jenna Johnson, "Majority of College Dropouts Cite Financial Struggles as Main Reason," *The Washington Post*, December 9, 2009.

9. The Public Policy Institute of California, *California Budget*, http://www.ppic.org/content/pubs/report/R_212MWR.pdf.

10. Stuart Anderson, "40 Percent of Fortune 500 Companies Founded by Immigrants or Their Children," *Forbes*, June 19, 2011.

11. John Steel Gordon, "The Man Who Saved the Cadillac," *Forbes*, May 1, 2009.

12. Yue Wang, "More People Have Cell Phones than Toilets," *Time Magazine*, March 25, 2013.

Chapter 3: Cracking the Code of Finance

1. Ariel Investments and Charles Schwab, *The Ariel/Schwab Black Investor Survey: Saving and Investing among Higher Income African-Americans and White Americans* (Hsinchu City, Taiwan: Argosy Research, 2008).

2. Andrew Young and Kabir Sehgal, *Walk in My Shoes: Conversations between a Civil Rights Legend and His Godson on the Journey Ahead* (New York: Palgrave Macmillan, 2010).

3. As seen in the Ford's Theatre museum in Washington, DC.

Chapter 4: Banking and Financial Services

1. United States Department of the Interior, National Park Service, *National Registry of Historic Places Inventory—Nomination Form,* http:// pdfhost.focus.nps.gov/docs/NHLS/Text/78000754.pdf.

2. Joseph Giovinco, "Democracy in Banking: The Bank of Italy and California's Italians," *California Historical Quarterly* 47, no. 3 (September 1968): 197.

3. Christine Bradley, Susan Burhouse, Heather Gratton, and Rae-Ann Miller, *Alternative Financial Services: A Primer* (Washington, DC: Federal Deposit Insurance Corporation, 2009).

4. Bank of America and Kahn Academy, "Better Money Habits," http://www.bettermoneyhabits.com/en/home.html#fbid=4pMltrfD_t6.

5. Federal Deposit Insurance Corporation, *2011 FDIC National Survey of Unbanked and Underbanked Households* (Washington, DC: Federal Deposit Insurance Corporation, 2012).

6. Stephanie Clifford and Jessica Silver-Greenberg, "Platinum Card and Text Alert, via Pawnshop," *The New York Times,* August 24, 2013.

Chapter 5: The Working Family's Hedge Fund

1. Nathan Bomey, Brent Snavely, and Alisa Priddle, "Detroit Becomes Largest U.S. City to Enter Bankruptcy," *Detroit Free Press,* December 3, 2013.

2. On average, people with a credit score in the 760 to 850 range will pay a full percentage point less interest on a thirty-year, $300,000 mortgage than will someone with a credit score of 620 to 639. Although the slightly increased monthly payments may not seem costly in the short term, people with lower credit scores pay significantly more over the life of the loan than those with better credit scores.

3. John Hope Bryant and Robert Gnaizda, "How to End the Homeownership Crisis," *American Banker,* October 25, 2012.

Chapter 6: 700 Credit Score Communities

1. Lisa J. Servon, "The Real Reason the Poor Go without Bank Accounts," *The Atlantic Cities,* September 11, 2013.

Chapter 7: The Power of Small Business and Entrepreneurship

1. Gallup and Operation HOPE, *2011 Gallup-HOPE Index,* available from http://www.operationhope.org.

2. Jim Clifton, "Dead Wrong: America's Economic Assumptions," *Gallup Business Journal,* March 21, 2013, http://businessjournal.gallup.com/content/161378/dead-wrong-america-economic-assumptions.aspx.

3. United States Department of Agriculture, Agricultural Marketing Service, "Food Deserts," http://apps.ams.usda.gov/fooddeserts/foodDeserts.aspx.

4. Gallup–HOPE Poll, 2013 results.

5. C. Chapman, J. Laird, N. Ifill, and A. Kewal Ramani, *Trends in High School Dropout and Completion Rates in the United States* (Washington, DC: U.S. Department of Education, 2011).

6. Jim Clifton, "Dead Wrong."

7. Malcolm Gladwell, *The Tipping Point: How Little Things Can Make a Big Difference* (New York: Little, Brown and Company, 2000).

8. Gallup and Operation HOPE, *2011 Gallup-HOPE Index.*

9. Sam Dillon, "Large Urban–Suburban Gap Seen in Graduation Rates," *The New York Times,* April 2, 2009.

10. Clive R. Belfield and Henry M. Levin, *The Economic Losses from High School Dropouts in California* (California Dropout Research Project Report no. 1, Santa Barbara, CA: University of California, Santa Barbara, 2007).

11. Clive R. Belfield, Henry M. Levin, and Rachel Rosen, *The Economic Value of Opportunity Youth* (New York: Columbia University and Queens College, 2012).

Chapter 8: The HOPE Plan

1. See President's Advisory Council on Financial Capability, "Final Report," January 29, 2013, http://blogs-images.forbes.com/amyrosen/files/2013/02/PACFC-final-report.pdf.

2. Federal Deposit Insurance Corporation, *2011 FDIC National Survey.*

3. Employer best practices to improve the financial literacy of their workforce are found in President's Advisory Council on Financial Capability, "Final Report." For details on the benefits to an employer that provides financial literacy education, see "Financial Literacy Tied to Productivity," *Employee Benefit News,* August 9, 2012.

4. Clive R. Belfield, Henry M. Levin, and Rachel Rosen, *The Economic Value of Opportunity Youth.*

5. Martin Luther King Jr., *Where Do We Go From Here: Chaos or Community?* (New York: Beacon Press, 1968).

Chapter 9: Project 5117

1. More information about Project 5117 can be found at www.operation hope.org/p5117.

Conclusion: Where We Go from Here

1. C. K. Prahalad, *The Fortune at the Bottom of the Pyramid: Eradicating Poverty through Profits* (Upper Saddle River, NJ: Prentice Hall, 2010).

2. Michael Greenstone and Adam Looney, "A Record Decline in Government Jobs: Implications for the Economy and America's Workforce," *Brookings on Job Numbers*, August 3, 2012.

ACKNOWLEDGMENTS

As a young man who grew up in Compton, California, who has spent his life investing in ideas filled with the promise of achieving and living the American dream, I have wanted to write this book for a long time. With that said, writing a book is like herding cats; you can rarely get all the ideas, perspectives, and active feedback moving in the same direction at once, or even pulled all into one space. But that's part of the magic of writing a book. When you keep an aggressive schedule, as any leader of a growing profit or not-for-profit organization would attest, you must be surrounded by amazing individuals who play the roles of supporter, advisor, fact checker, researcher, editor, agent, publisher, antagonizer, friend, coworker, prod-der, and sounding board to help you through the arduous pro-cess of getting your thoughts and ideas down on paper. I can assure you that I have tested the patience of all the individuals who have played one or more of these roles, and yet they were still there for me.

I'd like to thank my Operation HOPE board, employees, and team members, and the HOPE Corps volunteer family. In particular, special thanks to HOPE board members Jim M. Wells III, Bill Rogers, Jim Clifton (along with the entire

Gallup family), Steve Bartlett, Lynn Carter, Tim Chrisman, Tim Wennes, Duncan Niederauer, Philippe Bourguignon, William Hanna, Steve Ryan, Michael Shepherd, and Michael Arougheti. Love and appreciation to my personal chief of staff and confidant of twenty-one years, Rachael Doff, who supports me in every aspect of my life; as well as my executive and personal assistants, Leslie Alessandro, Charmela Freeman, and Sirjames Buchanon. And to the other key members of my senior management team, including Bill Walbrecher, Lance Triggs, Mary Hagerty Ehrsam, Frederick D. Smith, Jena Roscoe, Elaine Hungenberg, and James Bailey: thank you. Special thanks to Rod McGrew, my best friend, and to Tammy Edwards, both of whom read sections of this book along the way and provided me with their honest feedback.

Thank you to my publisher's visionary editorial director, Neal Maillet, who had faith in my idea for this book even before full understanding was achieved. For the incredible work of my development and copy editor, Todd Manza—thank you for your candor and discipline (smile). Todd gave order and structure to my unending mental thought processes.

To my personal editor, Kevin Morris, who engaged in the process in the final days of the book and did a stellar job making sure everything was tight and right and that the true message of the book would rise to the level of a work to be taken seriously by leaders around the world. And to my personal research assistant, Lucas Turner-Owens, who spent countless hours, day and night and on weekends, helping me make sure that the final book lived up to its promise, without ever once complaining. Thank you both. Others who provided important support to me throughout the publishing process include my agent, Pilar Queen, and members of the Berrett-Koehler family, including Michael Crowley, Kat Engh, Kylah Frazier, Zoe Mackey, David Marshall, Dianne Platner, Courtney Schonfeld, Katie Sheehan, Jeevan Sivasubramaniam, Richard Wilson, and Berrett-Koehler's president and publisher, Steve Piersanti.

My deep appreciation goes to the wisest men I have had the distinct honor of knowing and being mentored by. First is my play father, the Reverend Dr. Cecil "Chip" Murray, who basically raised me in my adult life; second is Ambassador Andrew Young (and his better half, Ms. Carolyn Young), civil rights icon and right-hand strategist to the late Dr. Martin Luther King Jr.; third is Quincy Jones, music legend, global citizen, and the epitome of what the spirit of entrepreneurship can do to transform America and our world; and, finally, South African Archbishop Emeritus Desmond Tutu, who believes in the kind of capitalism that prioritizes the needs of the many first, before the individual. Thanks for allowing me to call you "Arch" (smile). And to the daughter of Dr. Martin Luther King Jr., Dr. Bernice A. King: thank you for sharing your valuable point of view about your father's final mission to end poverty, the Poor People's Campaign.

I'm also grateful to the leaders who shared their wisdom and unique points of view around the issue of making free enterprise and capitalism work for the poor of any nation, but in America in particular, including Governor Tim Pawlenty, Mark Cassidy, Anand Nallathambi, Kent Stone, Jamie Dimon, Secretary Alphonso Jackson, Rick Smith, Johnnie Johns, Grayson Hall, Joseph Otting, Charles Schwab, Carrie Schwab Pomerantz, Gail McGovern, Thomas Guevara, Susan L. Taylor, Andrew "Bo" Young, Tom Neilssen, Steve Gillenwater,

Antoinette Malveaux, Tim Sloan, Tim Hanlon, Brad Blackwell, Tom Swanson, John Sotoodeh, Ajay Banga, Shawn Miles, Pierre Habis, Alex Cummings, Peter Ueberroth, William C. Bell, Diane Brady, Dan Mahurin, Christopher Ruddy, Soledad O'Brien, Van Jones, Ben Jealous, Richard Ketchum, Bill George, Professor Eldar Shafir, Atlanta Federal Reserve President Dennis Lockhart, Kansas City Federal Reserve President Esther George, Sheila Bair, Clare Woodcraft, Hasan Al-Jabri, Amr Ahmed Banaja, Karim Hajji, Luis Edson Feltrim, Kingsley Chiedu Moghalu, Professor Klaus Schwab, Professor Pekka Himanen, HRH Crown Prince Haakon Magnus of Norway, and President Bill Clinton.

Likewise, Sean Cleary, a senior advisor to the chairman at the World Economic Forum, helped me understand the plight of the world's poor in contrast to the poverty I have witnessed and lived firsthand in America. Sean has dedicated his life to shrinking the divide between the rich and the poor through his active involvement in policy creation. His knowledge, experience, and passionate leadership in growing the work of HOPE internationally inspire me.

Thank you to my family, including my mother, Juanita Smith; my father, Johnie W. Smith; my mother-in-law, Gwendolyn Foreman; my sisters and sister-in-law, Mara Lamont Hoskins, Arlene Hayes, and Alexandra Foreman; my brother, Dave D. Harris, and his family; my goddaughters, Kirstin Martinez and Jade Howard; and my son, Bishop Milo Bryant, a chocolate lab who loves me even when I am unlovable, as evidenced by his slobber and sitting on me with his ninety-pound body. And finally to my loving wife, Natasha Foreman Bryant, MBA, who not only provided the encouragement and active dialogue I needed to wrap my head around this sensitive topic but also helped to frame the issues in such a way that, hopefully, all who read this book will become inspired to get involved in bringing about change in our world. Thank you for your patience and for being a true partner. I am blessed to have found my equal—or better (smile).

For our nation's public servants, who continue to try to find the delicate (and sometimes seemingly impossible) balance between consumer financial access for all and banking innovation, financial regulation, institutional oversight, and consumer protection. I applaud you for your leadership and diligence in what is usually a pretty thankless job. Many leaders have been helpful in our work, including U.S. Federal Reserve Chairman Ben Bernanke; Federal Reserve System Chair–designate Janet Yellen; U.S. Comptroller Thomas J. Curry and OCC colleagues Paul Nash and Barry Wides; FDIC Chairman Martin J. Gruenberg, Vice Chairman Tom Hoenig, and other friends at the FDIC; Richard Cordray at the Consumer Financial Protection Bureau; and Cyrus Amir-Mokri, Don Graves, Melissa Koide, Louisa Quittman, and other friends at the U.S. Department of the Treasury.

Thank you, one and all. Let's go change the world, starting right now. Let's go . . .

INDEX

ABOUT OPERATION HOPE INC.

The mission of Operation HOPE Inc. is silver rights empowerment, making free enterprise work for everyone. We accomplish this through our work on the ground as the nonprofit
private banker for the working poor, the underserved, and the
struggling middle class. We achieve our mission by being the
best-in-class provider of financial literacy empowerment for
youth, financial capability for communities, and ultimately,
financial dignity for all.

Since its inception in 1992, HOPE has served more than two
million individuals. HOPE has also directed more than $1.5
billion in private capital to America's low-wealth communities,
maintains a growing army of twenty thousand HOPE Corps
volunteers, and currently serves more than three hundred
U.S. cities, as well as Morocco, Saudi Arabia, South Africa, and
the United Arab Emirates.

See more at http://www.operationhope.org.

ABOUT THE AUTHOR

John Hope Bryant is an entrepreneur, author, advisor, and one of the nation's most recognized empowerment leaders. He is the founder, chairman, and CEO of Operation HOPE and Bryant Group Companies, and, as the author of *Love Leadership: The New Way to Lead in a Fear-Based World* (Jossey–Bass, 2009), is the only African-American best-selling business author in America. Mr. Bryant serves for President Barack Obama as chairman of the President's Advisory Council on Financial Capability, Subcommittee on the Underserved and Community Empowerment.

Mr. Bryant is the cofounder of the Gallup–HOPE Index, the only national research poll on youth financial dignity and youth economic energy in the United States. He also is a cofounder of Global Dignity, with Crown Prince Haakon of Norway and Professor Pekka Himanen of Finland. Global Dignity is affiliated with the Forum of Young Global Leaders and the World Economic Forum.

Mr. Bryant is a thought leader represented by the Bright-Sight Group for public speaking and serves on the board of directors of Ares Commercial Real Estate Corporation (NYSE: ACRE), a specialty finance company managed by an affiliate of Ares Management LLC, a global alternative asset manager with approximately $59 billion in committed capital under management as of December 31, 2012.

Berrett–Koehler
Publishers

Berrett-Koehler is an independent publisher dedicated to an ambitious mission: *Creating a World That Works for All.*

We believe that to truly create a better world, action is needed at all levels—individual, organizational, and societal. At the individual level, our publications help people align their lives with their values and with their aspirations for a better world. At the organizational level, our publications promote progressive leadership and management practices, socially responsible approaches to business, and humane and effective organizations. At the societal level, our publications advance social and economic justice, shared prosperity, sustainability, and new solutions to national and global issues.

A major theme of our publications is "Opening Up New Space." Berrett-Koehler titles challenge conventional thinking, introduce new ideas, and foster positive change. Their common quest is changing the underlying beliefs, mindsets, institutions, and structures that keep generating the same cycles of problems, no matter who our leaders are or what improvement programs we adopt.

We strive to practice what we preach—to operate our publishing company in line with the ideas in our books. At the core of our approach is stewardship, which we define as a deep sense of responsibility to administer the company for the benefit of all of our "stakeholder" groups: authors, customers, employees, investors, service providers, and the communities and environment around us.

We are grateful to the thousands of readers, authors, and other friends of the company who consider themselves to be part of the "BK Community." We hope that you, too, will join us in our mission.

A BK Currents Book

This book is part of our BK Currents series. BK Currents books advance social and economic justice by exploring the critical intersections between business and society. Offering a unique combination of thoughtful analysis and progressive alternatives, BK Currents books promote positive change at the national and global levels. To find out more, visit **www.bkconnection.com**.

Berrett–Koehler
Publishers

A community dedicated to creating
a world that works for all

Dear Reader,

Thank you for picking up this book and joining our worldwide community of Berrett-Koehler readers. We share ideas that bring positive change into people's lives, organizations, and society.

To welcome you, we'd like to offer you a free e-book. You can pick from among twelve of our bestselling books by entering the promotional code BKP92E here: http://www.bkconnection.com/welcome.

When you claim your free e-book, we'll also send you a copy of our e-newsletter, the *BK Communiqué*. Although you're free to unsubscribe, there are many benefits to sticking around. In every issue of our newsletter you'll find

- A free e-book
- Tips from famous authors
- Discounts on spotlight titles
- Hilarious insider publishing news
- A chance to win a prize for answering a riddle

Best of all, our readers tell us, "Your newsletter is the only one I actually read." So claim your gift today, and please stay in touch!

Sincerely,

Charlotte Ashlock
Steward of the BK Website

Questions? Comments? Contact me at bkcommunity@bkpub.com.

Certified

B

Corporation
bcorporation.net

CPSIA information can be obtained at www.ICGtesting.com
Printed in the USA
BVOW04*1649170614

356623BV00001B/1/P